The JOY of DRAWING

A BEGINNER'S MANUAL

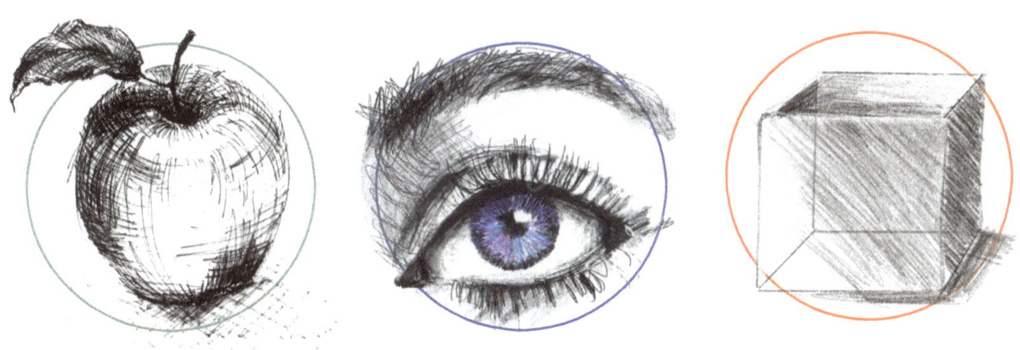

Caroline Mustard
& Katy Lea

We are dedicating
this book to those
who joined our
earliest drawing
classes: Karen
Kotoske, Cheryl
Branco, Sarah, Kim,
Haideh, Hanna,
Hilary and all of
our students past,
present and future,
Thank you.
This book is for you,

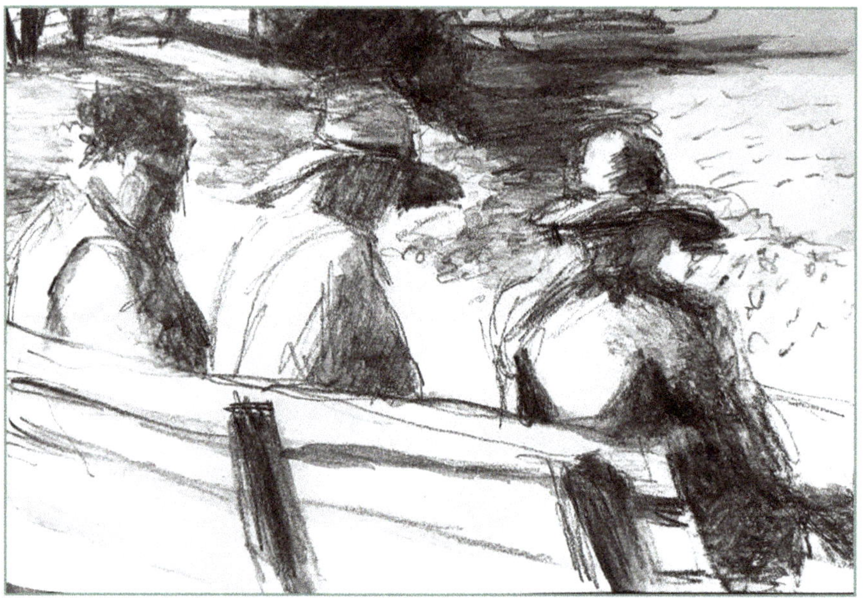

Table of Contents

Chapter	Title	Page
	Preface	5
1	The Fundamentals	9
2	Textures and Patterns	19
3	Shading and Shadows	29
4	Gridding	37
5	Charcoal	43
6	Shapes and Forms	47
7	Proportions	59
8	Drawing without a Net	65
9	Sketching	73

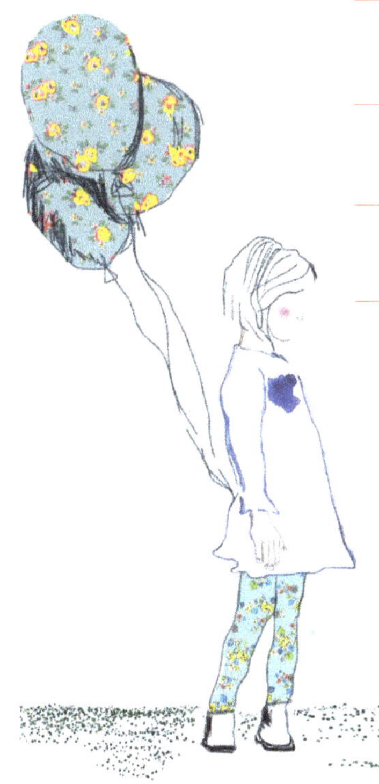

My love of drawing began when I was a child growing up in rural England. This is an example of an early sketch. Both Katy and I had the chance to perfect our drawing skills early on in life and now we want to pass those fundamentals on to you in the forthcoming chapters.

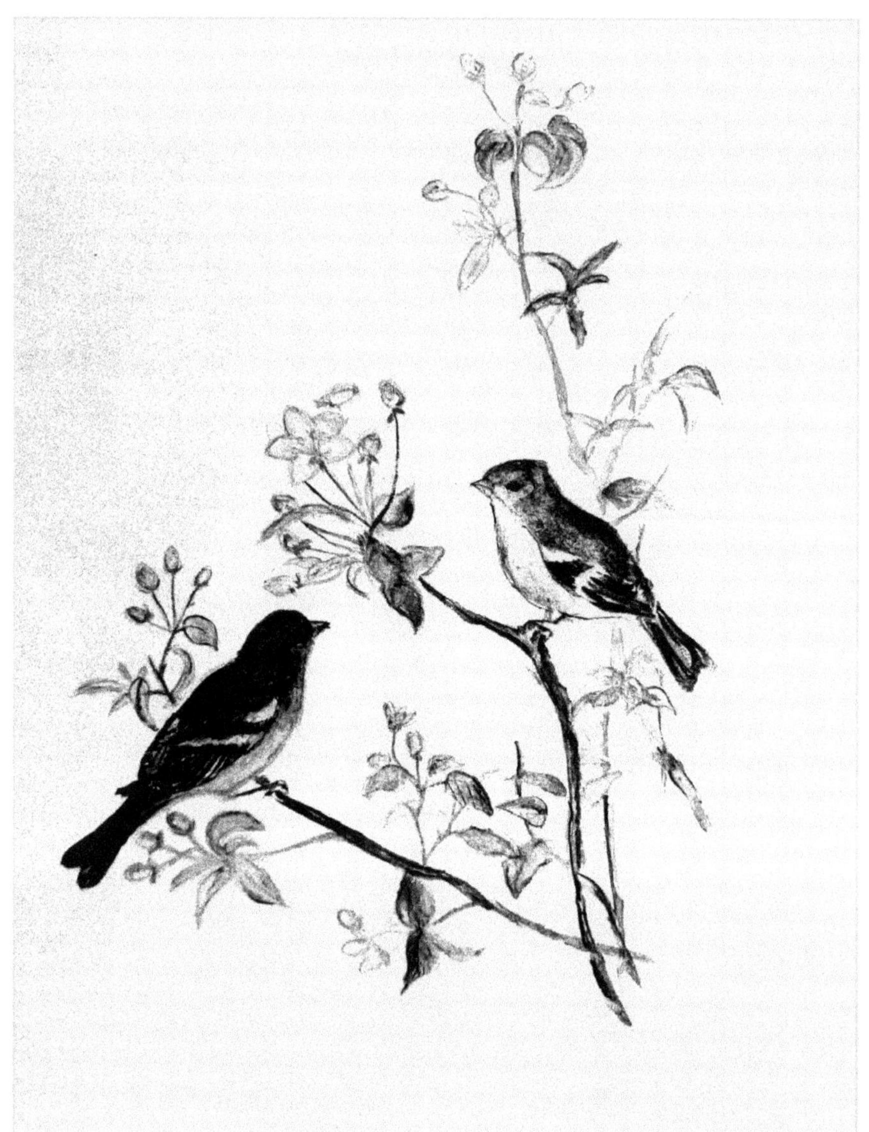

Preface

I can remember the first drawing that satisfied me. I was sitting in my beloved Grandma's kitchen, drawing the stork that adorned the Stork Margarine packet in post World War II Great Britain (we were on strict rationing). My drawing looked just like the stork and I was inordinately proud of my accomplishment.

My earliest disappointment occurred when I drew my first portrait. I found a round jam-jar top and drew around it for my head. When I proudly showed my friend Hermione Bird, her older sister Joanna showed me her portrait drawing. I was devastated; I realized I had it entirely wrong (which she didn't hesitate to point out). Her head was egg-shaped and looked like a head and mine didn't.

So I practiced and practiced. I copied all my favorite illustrations from Winnie the Pooh. I drew all the little model animals from my prized collection. At the tender age of five, I had a lot of time on my hands – I was forced to spend months in isolation due to contracting infantile tuberculosis. My mother created a nursery for me full of pencils, paper, and watercolor paints. It also didn't hurt that I was an only child looking for ways to entertain myself, or that I lived deep in the countryside where I could take long walks and collect wildflowers to take home and draw in quiet solitude. And, of course, I never stopped. There was never a question of what I was going to do with my life. So here I am today, sharing my joy of drawing with you.

I am happy to say I am joined by my good friend Katy who, like me, grew up in rural Britain (some three decades later than I!) And, like me, Katy learned by copying; sitting together with her elder sister drawing at the kitchen table on anything she could get her hands on — newspapers, sweet wrappers, cornflake boxes and the like.

While attending Art school in the 60's I was lucky enough to have a traditional teacher; he became my hero and gave me the best advice, which I now forward on to you: If you want

"Drawing is the root of everything, and the time spent on that is actually all profit."
Vincent van Gogh

AHA!
When learning to draw, the word "copy" is not a 4-letter word!

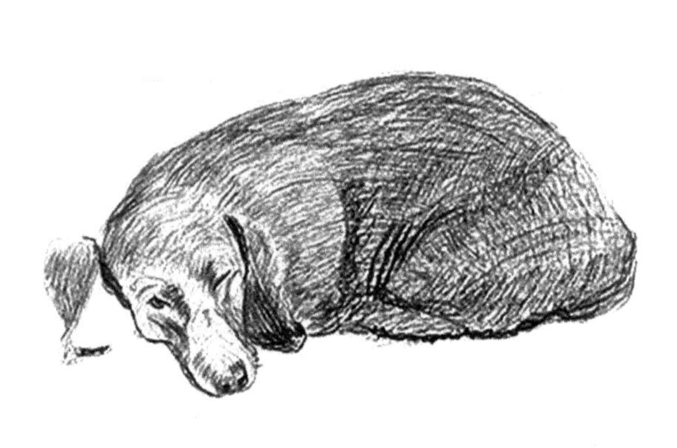

David Hockney, "Stanley" (1993)

"I was aware that the teaching of drawing was being stopped almost 30 years ago. And I always said, 'The teaching of drawing is the teaching of looking.' A lot of people don't look very hard. "
David Hockney

to be an artist you have to draw and draw and draw, you simply have to draw every day. You have to carry a sketchbook everywhere and you have to look, look, look. Don't worry about the results. It's the journey that is important, not the destination.

So I did just that: I drew while I queued up with my pals waiting to see 'The Beatles' or sitting on the bus going back and forth to art school, or hiking through the hills and dales in the Cotswolds, sketching the magical landscape. Katy had similar experiences, and an art teacher who gave her the same advice - to keep a sketchbook near her and to copy the world around her.

We both realized that not everyone had that opportunity or got the basic training and guidance that we received which helped us both master the skill of drawing. And, it is a skill. You learn it like you learn to cook or ride a bike. And if you are learning it late in life, no worries. Van Gogh and Gauguin and even Kandinsky started late in life without formal art education in their youth, and they did pretty well! And, guess what, they learned to draw FIRST and they learned to draw by copying just as all the great masters did before them. So take heart.

In both cases, the road Katy and I traveled led to our wanting to share our joy of drawing with others and teach them the skills we were so lucky to have learned early in life.

It all started when one of my students invited Katy and me to join her at Shoreline Lake Park in Mountain View, California to do some sketching. Neither of us had done much traditional drawing since leaving art school. We reveled in the joy of it, along with the fresh air and the wonderful view. On the way home, we dreamed up the idea of starting an 'Art Hiking' activity and inviting people to join us to take nature walks around the Shoreline Lake, while teaching them to draw.

We had to plan out what we needed to teach people, and to do that we had to figure out what the sequence of lessons should be. We went back to basics, finding the things other art teachers seldom taught, like, how to hold your pencil, the different types of pencils, and the very basics of mark making. So many "AHA!" moments for us and for our students.

Our experience showed us, time after time, that when one of our students felt they couldn't draw it led straight back to moments when they were intimidated; when their teacher passed by their work while praising a fellow student, making them want to give up. These moments tend to stick around as failures. We had to gently coax our students through their reluctance to make mistakes. We achieved this by helping them to take small steps and achieve victories in each lesson, until they finally could draw on their own, without any net.

In this series of lessons we want to guide you right from the beginning to gradually build your skill level whilst having some fun! So, take a deep relaxing breath, and let's get started on this amazing journey!

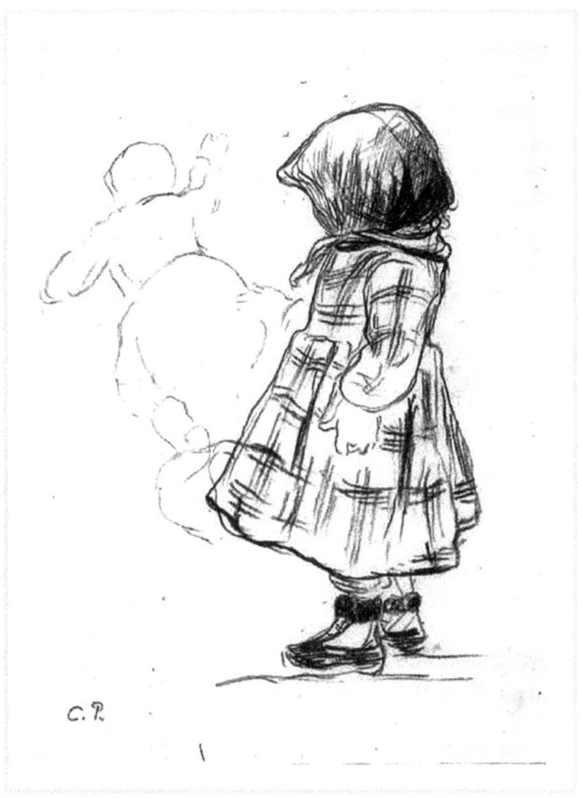

Camille Pissarro, "Jeune Garçon" (1883)

"It is only by drawing often, drawing everything, drawing incessantly, that one fine day you discover, to your surprise, that you have rendered something in its true character."
Camille Pissarro

FREE WORKBOOK & VIDEO DEMONSTRATIONS

For additional assistance we are providing you with free access to our printable Joy of Drawing Workbook as well as video demonstrations of each of the exercises for chapter. Use the QR codes below to access these free tools .

Joy of Drawing Workbook

Traditional drawing video demonstrations

Digital drawing video demonstrations

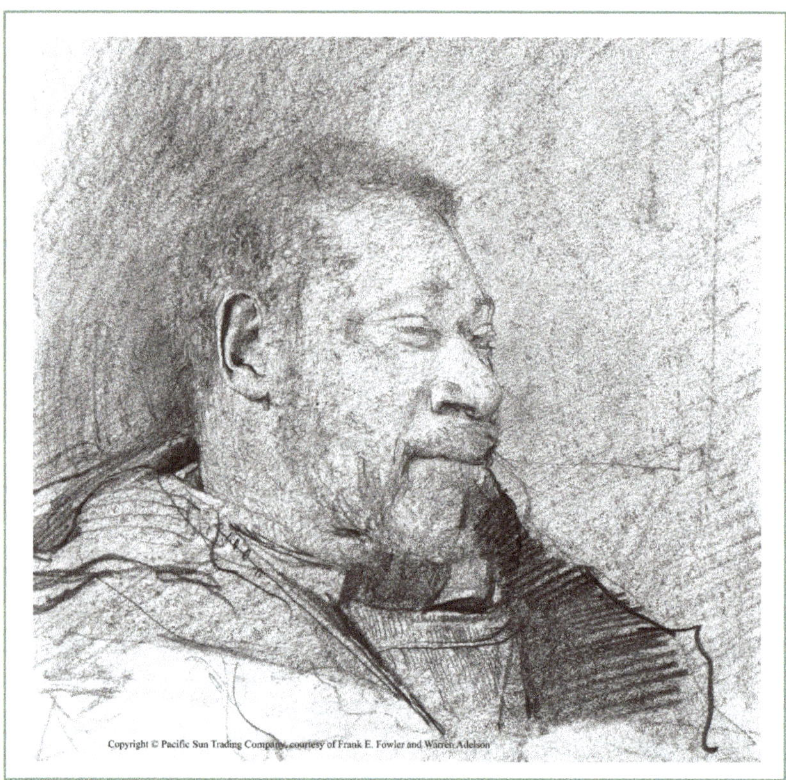
Copyright © Pacific Sun Trading Company, courtesy of Frank E. Fowler and Warren Adelson

Andrew Wyeth "Study for Grape Wine" (1966)

"I love the quality of pencil. It helps me to get to the core of a thing." Andrew Wyeth

Materials you will need for this book

- Graphite pencils in the basic grades: minimally HB, 2B, and 6B

- Kneaded eraser and regular eraser

- Pencil sharpener

- Charcoal

- Tortillons or blending stumps

- 60lb sketching paper

- 70-80lb drawing paper for the final exercise in each chapter

Chapter I: The Fundamentals

Like many people who began drawing when they were very young, Katy and I realized that there were certain things that we both naturally do that we both take for granted, and guess what? When we searched online, it seems that most other artists do the same.

We realized that the FUNDAMENTALS are missing from the most basic of art lessons, without which the lessons do not work and you will start off on the wrong foot.

So here they are. They may seem obvious. But, when you carry out these exercises, I think you will agree that these produce some surprising "AHA!" moments.

"A line is a dot that went for a walk...
A drawing is taking a line for a walk."
 Paul Klee

EXERCISE 1:
All Pencils are NOT the same!

Open your box of pencils and turn them around so you can see the letters on the side. You will notice they are different. Pencil manufacturers rank pencils on a grading scale from hard to soft. There are two grading systems for pencils - American and European. The American system is numerical and goes from 1 to 4, while the European system uses the letters "H" and "B" to note how hard or soft a pencil is.

Here is a doodling exercise that you can do to see how differently these types of pencils perform. Do not worry if you do not have each of these types of pencils. Simply line up the pencils you have in sequence per the chart displayed above.

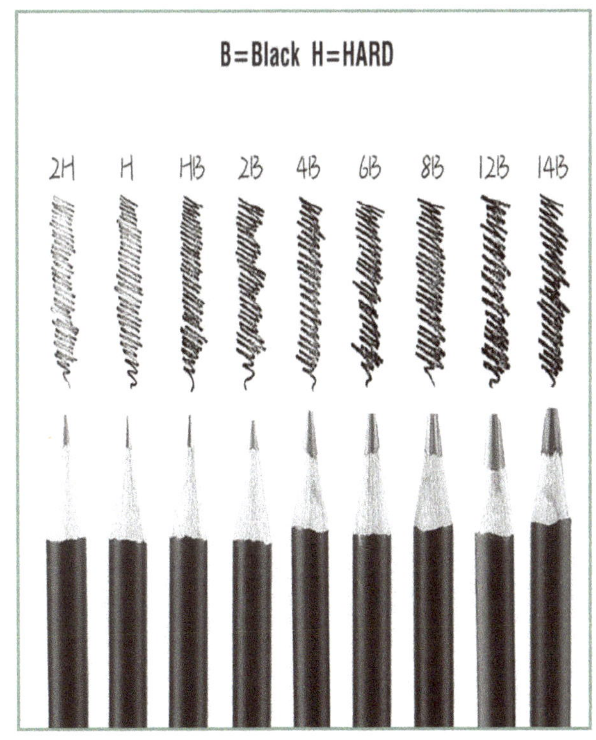

Put a piece of rough paper in front of you. Select the pencil with the hardest designation. Doodle on your paper with this pencil. Select the next pencil in line and repeat the exercise using EACH of the pencils.

When you are done, take your finger and rub over the pencil marks, notice the softer the pencil, the easier it is to smear.

If you watch an experienced artist you will notice they constantly change the way they hold their pencil to produce different types of lines and effects.

EXERCISE 2:
How to hold your pencil

When you write with a pencil, you may notice you hold it in a particular way. You don't even really think about it.

But where and how you hold your pencil has everything to do with the different types of lines you can create.

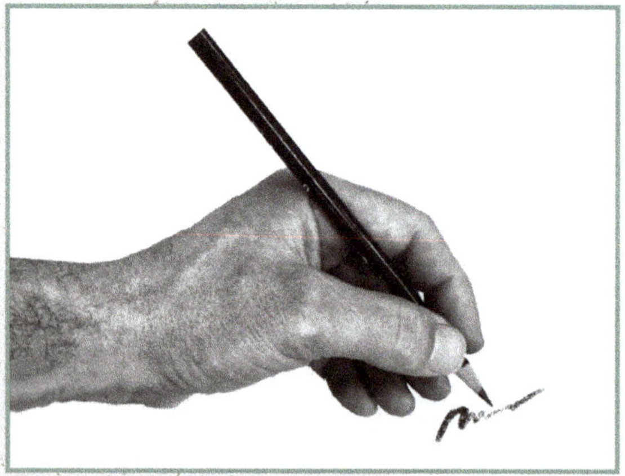

Traditional Grip (also known as the Tripod Grip)

This is the way most of us hold our pencil to write, and it works. However, it only works for writing and detailed drawing. Did you know there are FOUR other ways which artists use to draw different types of lines. Practice holding your pencil in each way and doodle with the pencil to see how it changes the character of the lines you are drawing.

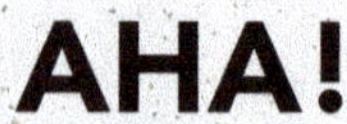

AHA!

You can create different types of marks just by changing the way you hold your pencil!

Drumstick Grip

This grip is very similar to how one should hold a drumstick. The pencil is held loosely between the index finger and the thumb, while the other fingers act to stabilize the pencil. Holding the pencil in this manner allows for the marks to originate from the side of the exposed graphite (or charcoal, or colored pencil) by laying it flat against the paper, instead of the just the tip.

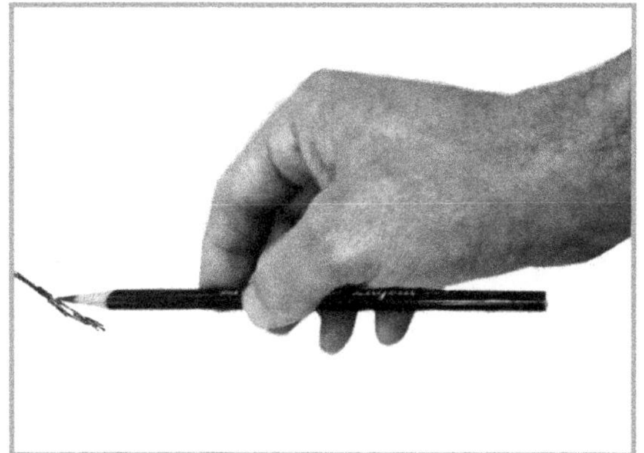

Paintbrush Grip

Here the pencil is held in a similar manner to holding a paint brush. The pencil is held upright and the back edge rests on the crease between your index finger and the base of your thumb. Generally the tip of the pencil is what makes contact on the drawing surface. Perfect for creating light and delicate marks.

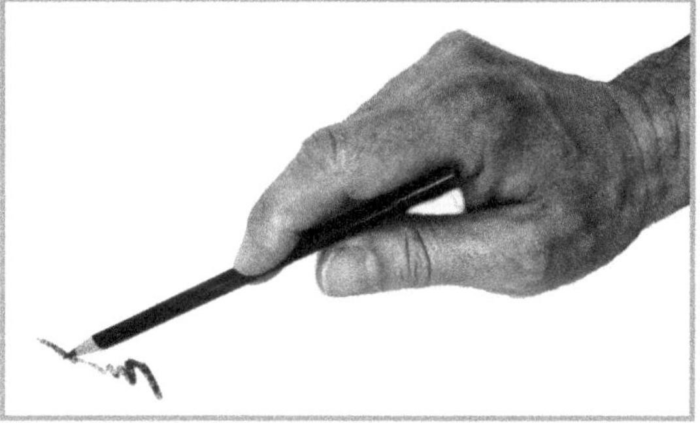

Top Heavy Grip

The midsection of the pencil is held between the middle finger and the thumb while pressure is exerted onto the tip of the pencil. The pencil lays almost parallel to the drawing surface, forcing the side of the tip of the pencil to make contact. The result is a strong mark that has potential for width variance. This grip is great for filling in large areas quickly. This grip also forces the use of the shoulder in the drawing process.

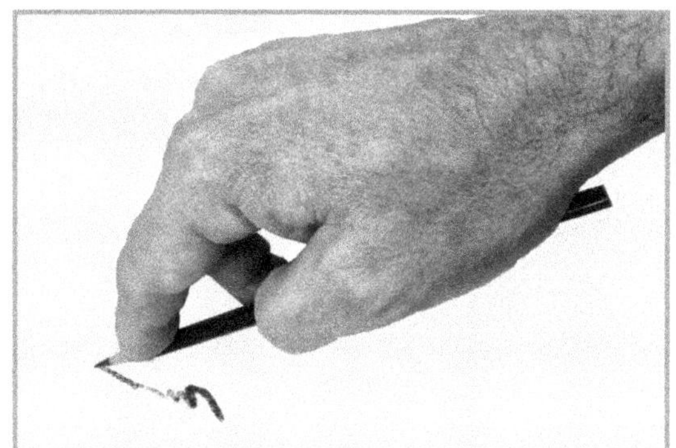

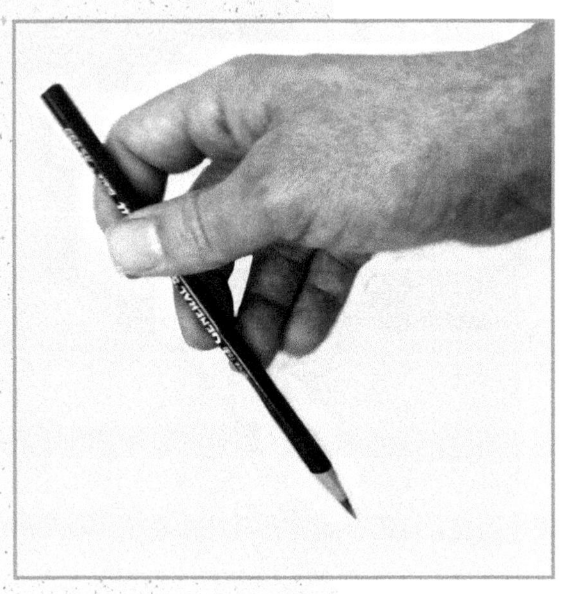

Inverted Grip

For this grip, the pencil is held by resting it upon the forefinger and stabilizing it with the thumb and lower fingers. The pencil should actually point back towards the artist. Marks are made with the tip and the backside of the tip of the pencil. This grip allows the artist to clearly see the marks as they are made since the hand and the fingers are out of the way.

You will notice as you change your grip that you are using different muscles to move the pencil around. Detailed drawing with the traditional grip uses mostly the finger muscles, while the others use the wrist, elbow and even the shoulder!

EXERCISE 3:
How to draw a straight line

We learned this exercise from an online lesson. It gave us an "AHA!" moment that we immediately realized was quite critical.

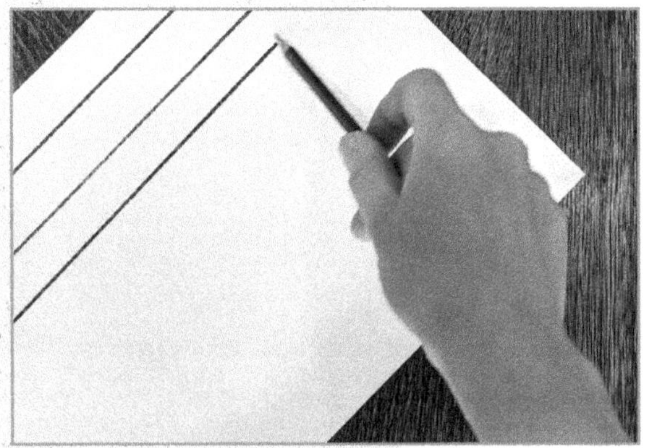

Few of us are gifted with the skill to draw straight lines. Using a ruler can make drawing look rather stilted, so being able to draw straight lines is crucial to a successful drawing.

If you are right handed, notice that, when you extend your arm from the elbow, it moves from lower left to upper right in a diagonal movement We call this your natural sweep. If you are left handed, you do the opposite; Lower right to upper left.

Instead of trying to draw straight lines while keeping your paper firmly in front of you, try moving the paper at an angle so it matches the direction of your natural sweep as shown in the photo. Now rapidly draw lines just by letting your hand move from left to right. Voilá! You have created some reasonably straight lines which go in the same direction, (lefties you would just place the paper the other way and go from right to left!)

Next, crisscross the paper with straight lines, but wait:

DO NOT try to change the direction of the sweep of your hand. INSTEAD just turn the paper around and keep moving your hand in its natural sweep.

Keep turning the paper and pretty quick you will have covered it with a crisscross of straight lines. They may not be completely straight, but they are way more accurate than anything you could have done using any other method.

EXERCISE 4:
How to draw curved lines

The next type of line is curved. Let's draw a few other types of lines starting with the "S" curve.

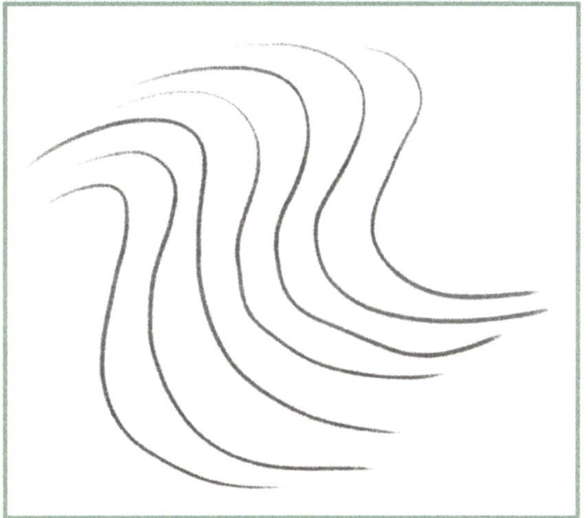

Place your paper in front of you and hold your pencil with the paintbrush grip and make a fast "S" shape. Do this a number of times and notice you are using your wrist to create this shape, while before you were using your elbow for the straight lines. Practice making large "S" curves now by just moving your elbow. Try a few other curvy shapes until you can easily draw nice curvy lines.

How to draw circles

Next we will move onto drawing circles which can be quite a challenge. Did you know that the famous Renaissance artist, Giotto, could draw a perfect circle? In fact he apparently used to draw a perfect circle, or so legend has it.

I noticed that when I draw a circle I go around and around to create the shape I finally want. But that's me.

We researched the subject on the internet and again found

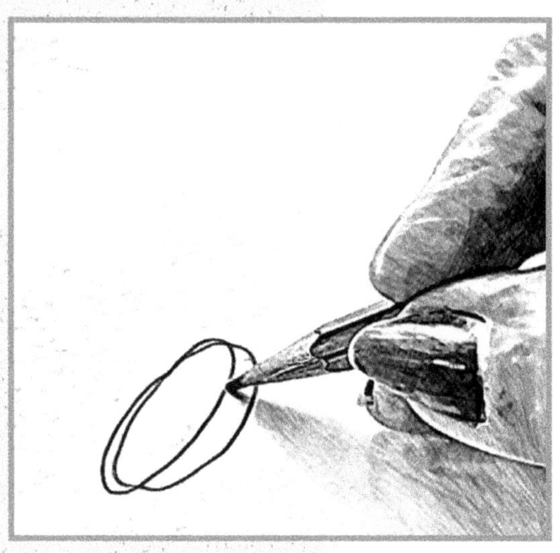

the best description for drawing a circle with just your pencil was from *'The Virtual Instructor'* which gives excellent directions in a way you can easily learn and, with practice, start to draw great circles or ellipses every time you need them.

First of all, you have to ask yourself this question: Why is it so hard to draw a circle?

When most of us try to draw a circle, we usually hold the pencil in a traditional grip, moving only our fingers and wrist. The result is usually an oval - not a circle - as pictured in this illustration.

Why is this? Well, your wrist has a limited range of motion. You can only make your wrist move so far in a circular motion before your control is sacrificed.

So therefore, we know that a near perfect circle cannot be achieved by just using our wrist. So, let's move a little higher up on the arm to our next joint - the elbow. Our elbow provides a little more flexibility when we use it in conjunction with our wrist. But we're still too limited to draw a circle.

The Secret to Drawing Great Circles

We have to move all the way up to the shoulder to see the range of movement required to draw a circle. The shoulder is a ball and socket joint. This type of connection allows for a broader range of movement. It's this joint where we find the range of motion required to draw the elusive circle. So although it may seem strange, you should draw your circles with your shoulder instead of your wrist or elbow.

In fact, you should try to lock your wrist and only move your elbow minimally. The majority of motion should come from your shoulder.

Even with your shoulder involved, you may find it difficult to draw a great circle with just one mark.

Imagine throwing darts at a dart board, that you had just one dart and you had to hit the bull's-eye with one attempt. Your chances of success would be pretty low.

But what if you had lots of darts and only one of them had to hit the bull's-eye. Your chances of success are now much greater. So, instead of drawing just one line to create a circle, why not draw several and then pull out your circle from the collection of lines you create.

Here's how it works:

Start with your pencil in hand hovering over the surface of the paper. Begin slowly moving your shoulder in circular motion without your pencil touching the surface. Your elbow may move slightly, but try to keep your wrist locked in place.

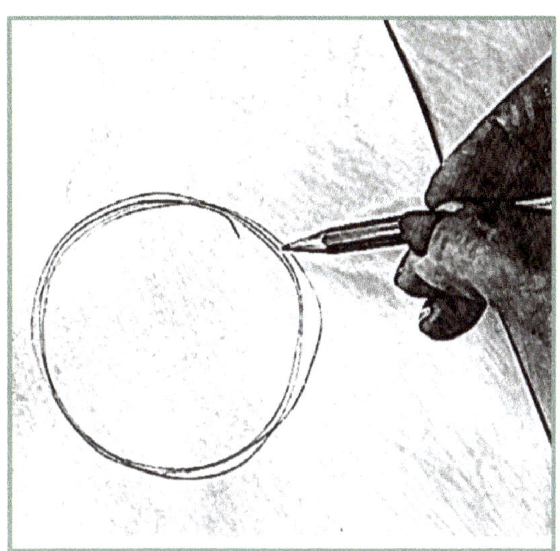

Lower your arm onto the surface while continuing to move your shoulder in a circular motion. Allow your pencil to make contact with the surface of the paper while your arm and shoulder continues to move. Make several light circular strokes on the drawing paper. until you have a collection of light circles.

These light circles will serve as guidelines over which you can trace a more refined circle, increasing the pressure on your pencil to do so. If you wish, you can use an eraser to clean up the guidelines.

This approach requires a little practice to perfect. The more you practice drawing circles in this way, the better you'll get at it. It just may take a little time to train your shoulder to work this way. But once you've got it down, you can draw circles whenever you need to and of whatever size you want them to be.

FINAL EXERCISE:
Drawing is relaxing and fun

Using a high quality piece of paper, cut it up into squares. For example If you are using a 9"x12" drawing pad you will get 12 3-inch squares altogether.

Take the first square and crisscross it with lines to divide it

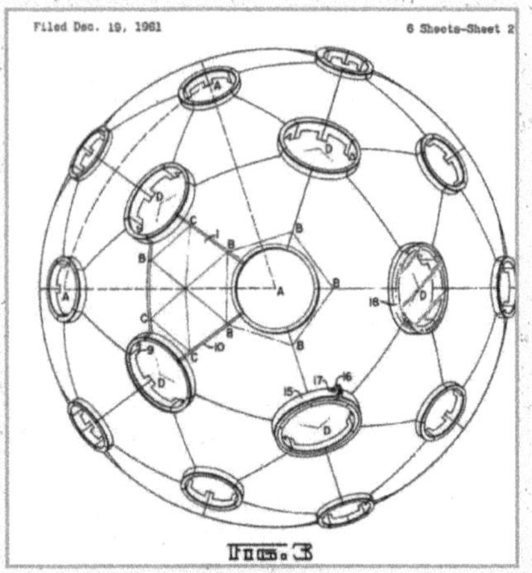

Buckminster Fuller "Patent Drawing for Geodesic Structure" (Aug 3, 1965)

"Whenever I draw a circle, I immediately want to step out of it." Buckminster Fuller

This lovely image was shared by student Connie who gave us the background to her drawing as follows: "What a terrific way to "rediscover" The JOY of Drawing. Doing this "Doodle" provided the opportunity to recall how Western Native Americans would place a sick person on the sand, then around that person, pour specific patterns of colored sand so as to HEAL the hurting community-member. Because of this centuries-old practice, I used a sandy colored Paper." C.F.

into shapes. Fill in each shape with a different pattern.

We've included some sample patterns on the next page. You can find more patterns by opening Google and searching for doodle patterns or Zentangle[R] patterns.

Carefully fill each shape with a different pattern.

Take your time, relax and enjoy the practice of drawing. This is a very relaxing meditation exercise you can do, perhaps in the evening while the TV is on. It requires you to be in the moment and hopefully will be your first introduction to the meditative value of drawing!

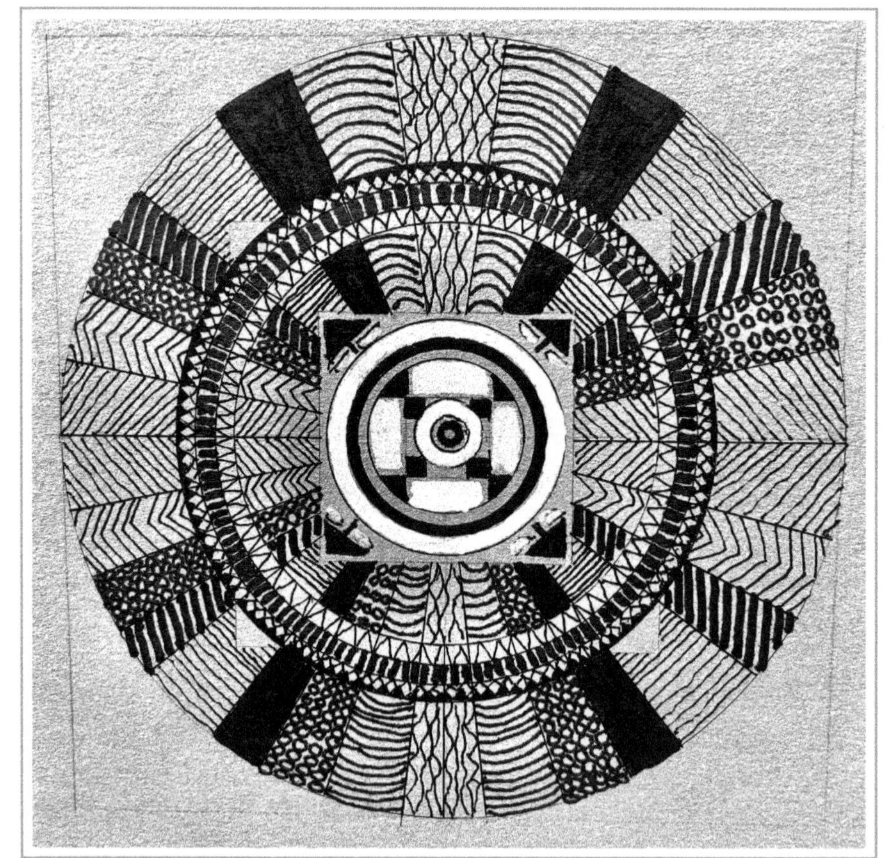

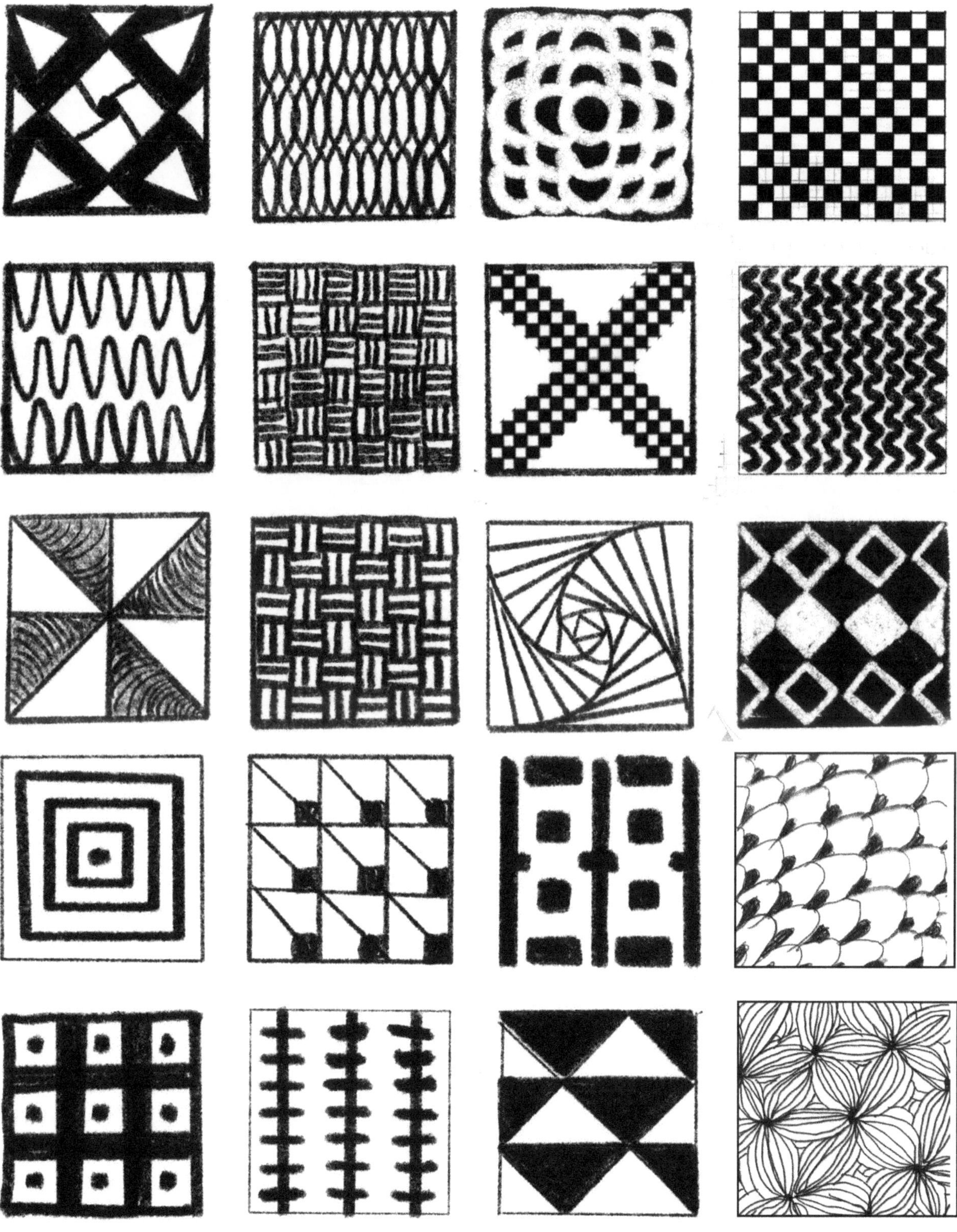

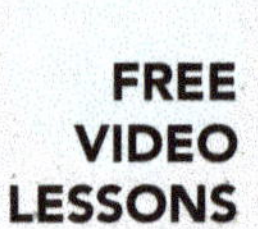

FREE VIDEO LESSONS

Traditional Drawing Video Demonstrations

FREE VIDEO LESSONS

Digital Drawing Video Demonstrations

FREE WORKBOOK DOWNLOAD

Your workbook contains all the images you need to complete the exercises in this chapter.

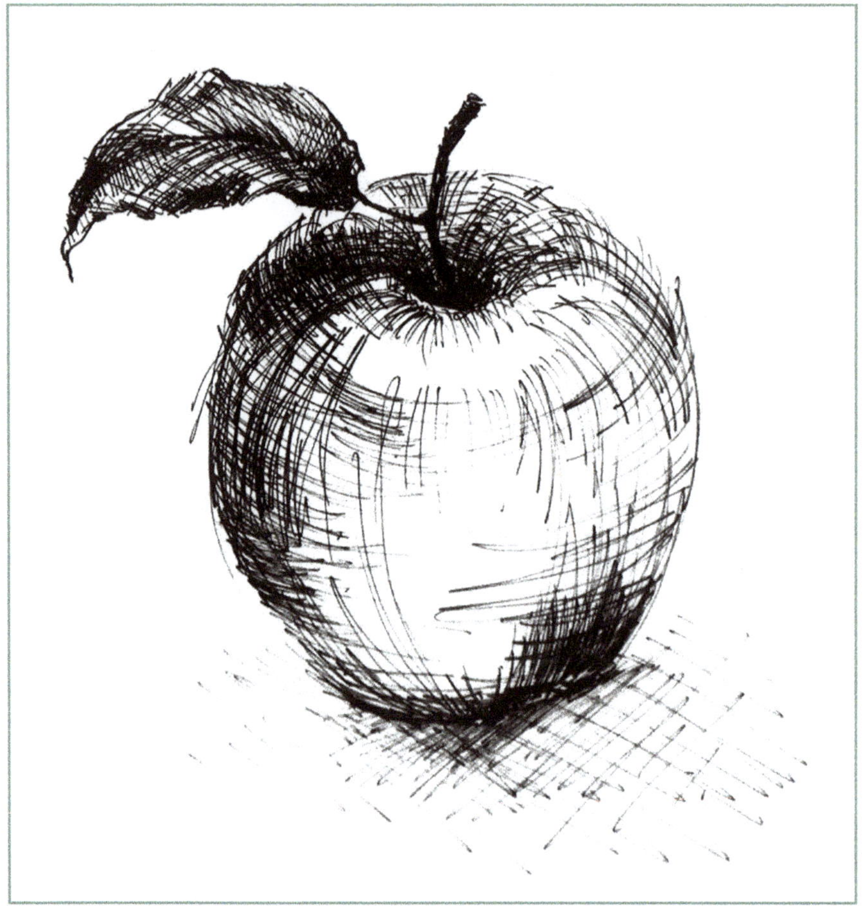

This drawing by Katy of an apple demonstrates the use of cross hatching, one of the techniques covered in this chapter.

Chapter 2: Textures and Patterns

From the earliest drawings in the Lascaux Caves to the graffiti artist in your local city, from the 2 year old scribbling on the table to Leonardo da Vinci; drawing is a process of mark making.

In this lesson we are going to learn that different types of marks create contrasting types of textures, each of which have a rather unique character and enable you to create differing tonal or shading effects.

We are highlighting five textures that have been used by artists down the ages. We have included an example of an artist's work to illustrate each of these five techniques.

The final exercise invites you to create some simple drawings using each technique so you get your own hands-on view of how to do it!

Drawing is still basically the same as it has been since prehistoric times. It brings together man and the world. It lives through magic."
Keith Haring

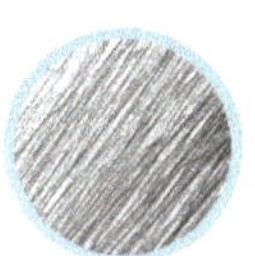

Hatching

Hatching is an artistic technique used to create tonal or shading effects by drawing closely spaced parallel lines, drawing the lines at differently spaced intervals and/or by altering the pressure on your pencil to create light or dark strokes. Using this technique allows you to create a graduated shading effect as seen in this example.

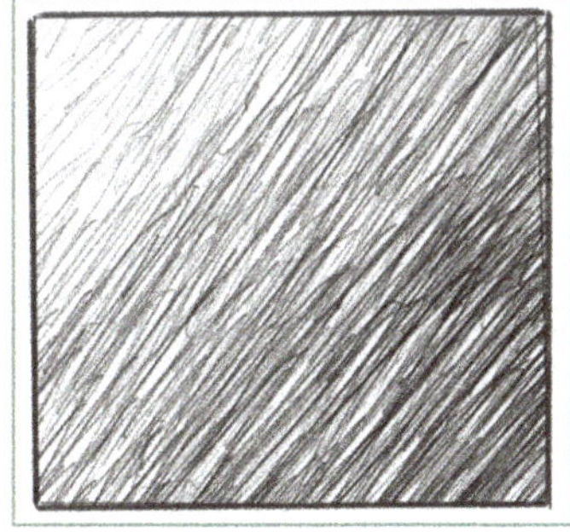

Hatching exercise:

1. Draw a square in your sketchbook and fill it with lines.

2. Draw a second box and this time space the lines differently from far apart to close to each other to create a gradually shaded box.

Claude Monet "L'Église de Varengeville; soleil couchant" (1883)

1. Draw a third box, and this time draw all the lines but alter the pressure on your pencil from light to dark.

2. Do this as often as you want until you feel comfortable with the technique then move on to the next one.

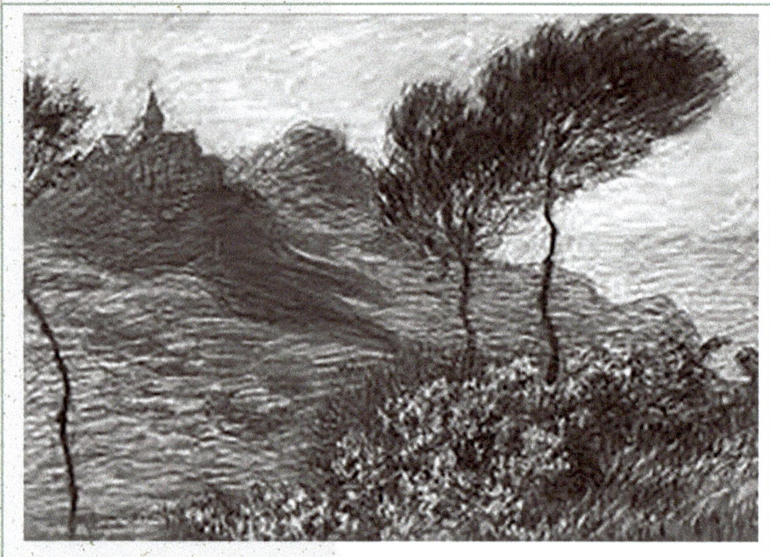

This drawing by Claude Monet demonstrates the use of hatching. Notice that the artist hatches different surfaces in different directions. In other words, you do not have to make all the lines go in the same direction.

You'll get a chance to do your own drawing using this method later in the chapter!

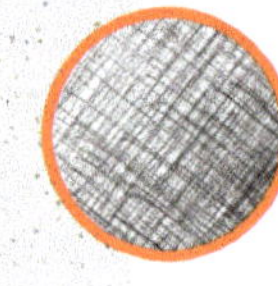

Cross hatching

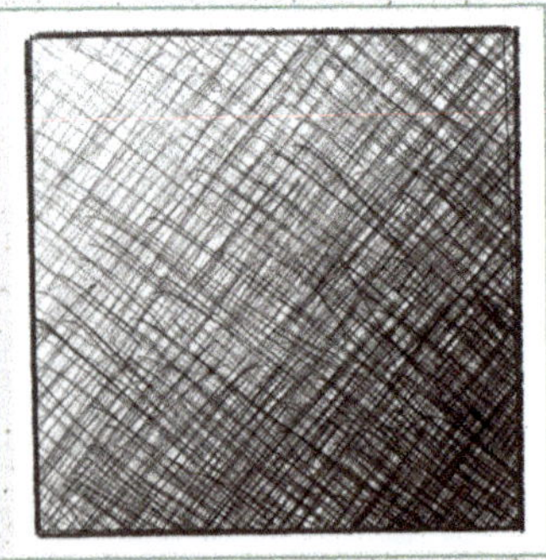

Cross hatching is an artistic technique used to create tonal or shading effects by drawing closely spaced lines placed at an angle to one another. You can see the example here. Again, you can change the pressure on your pencil to create light cross hatching lines to heavy lines, and thus graduate the shaded area from light to dark or vice versa.

Cross hatching exercise

1. Draw a square in your drawing book and fill with lines that crisscross each other.

2. Draw a second box and this time vary the pressure you put on the pencil to create a gradual increase from light to dark or vice versa.

3. Do this as often as you want until you feel comfortable then move on to the next one.

This drawing by Rembrandt demonstrates the use of cross hatching. Notice the lines can be curved, but the artist crisscrosses each line to create shadows, some lines are light while others are dark, showing the artist adjusts pressure on the pencil.

There are many other examples of this technique that you can find by searching cross hatching drawings on your search engine and viewing them in Images mode. You will get your own chance to use this technique in a simple drawing exercise at the end of this Chapter.

"Try to put well in practice what you already know; and in so doing, you will in good time, discover the hidden things you now inquire about. Practice what you know, and it will help to make clear what now you do not know".

Rembrandt van Rijn

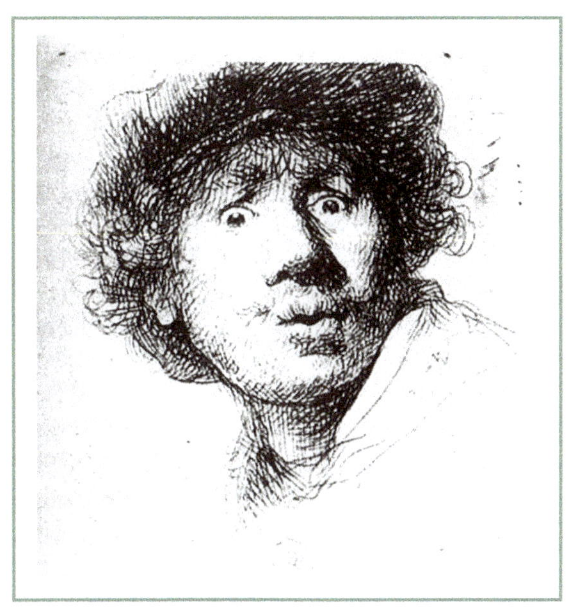

Rembrandt van Rijn "Self Portrait" (1630)

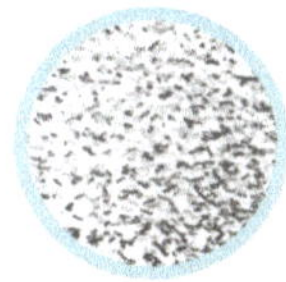

Pointillism or stippling

Pointillism or stippling is an artistic style for creating tonal or shading effects using only dots. This is more easily achieved using an ink pen or marker, but can be done with a blunted pencil.

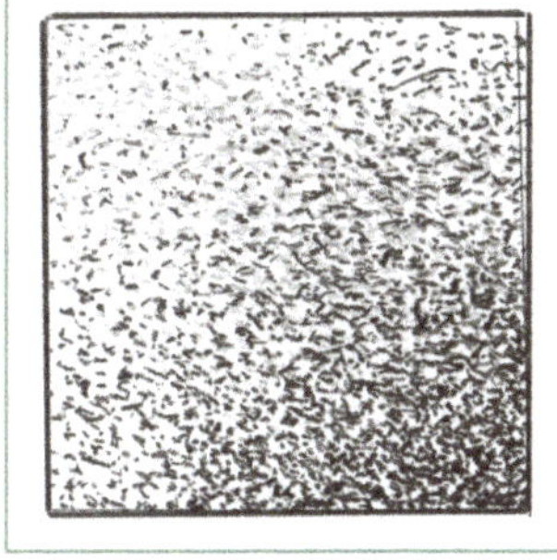

Pointillism Exercise

1. Draw a box in your drawing pad and fill it with dots using a blunt soft pencil or better still a brush pen or marker.

2. Draw a second box and this time space them apart at one corner of the square and then space them closer as you reach the other side to get a graduated tone from light to dark.

3. Do this as often as you like until you feel you have a good grasp of the technique.

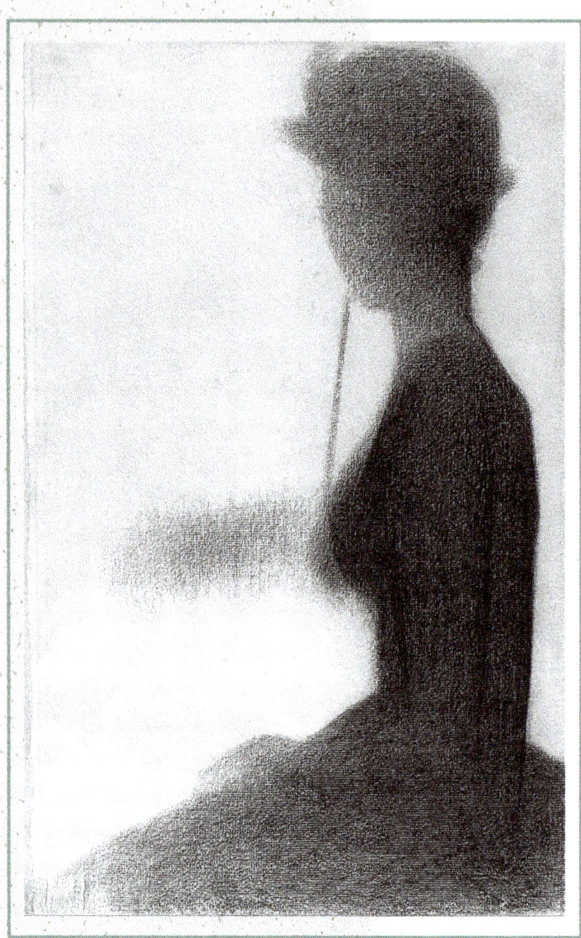

George Seurat "Seated Woman with a Parasol (study for La Grande Jatte)" (1884/85)

This charcoal drawing by George Seurat; an artist known for pioneering the use of small dots of pure color in his paintings. This approach became known as pointillism (although this was not what he called it!) This drawing is an example of using small marks to create tonal values. There are many other examples that you can research on the web.

"Originality depends only on the character of the drawing and the vision peculiar to each artist."
George Seurat

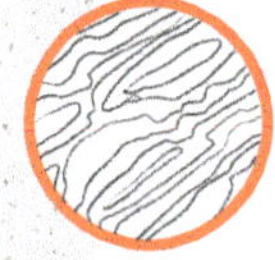 # Contouring or line drawing

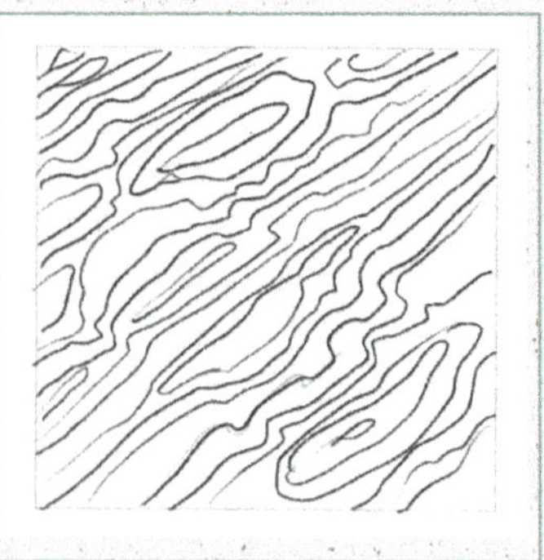

This is an artistic technique using lines to define the shape of objects, It is also used to create patterns seen in nature, and is used to show tonal value by drawing lines closer together to denote darker tones or by using pressure on the pencil to draw darker or lighter lines.

Contouring technique exercises

1. Draw a box and fill it with contour lines similar to those in this illustration.

2. Now draw a new box and change pressure you place on your pencil to create lighter and darker lines and observe the effects.

Blind contouring exercise

This is an exercise used by many artists to loosen them up.

1. Look around you for something that has obvious shapes such as a table with objects on it.

2. Using your sketchbook and without looking at your paper at all, trace the contours of what you see, while moving your pencil continuously. Do not worry about what it looks like on the paper or if you are accurate. Concentrate on what you are seeing and move your pencil according to the shapes you see.

3. Repeat this exercise often. You might get some unusual results as you build up your hand-eye coordination.

This portrait of Francoise Gilot by Pablo Picasso is a great example of how expressive contour drawing can be.

You will get a chance to experiment with this technique at the end of the chapter!

"Learn the rules like a pro,
so you can break them
like an artist."
Pablo Picasso

Pablo Picasso
"Francois Gilot" (1946)

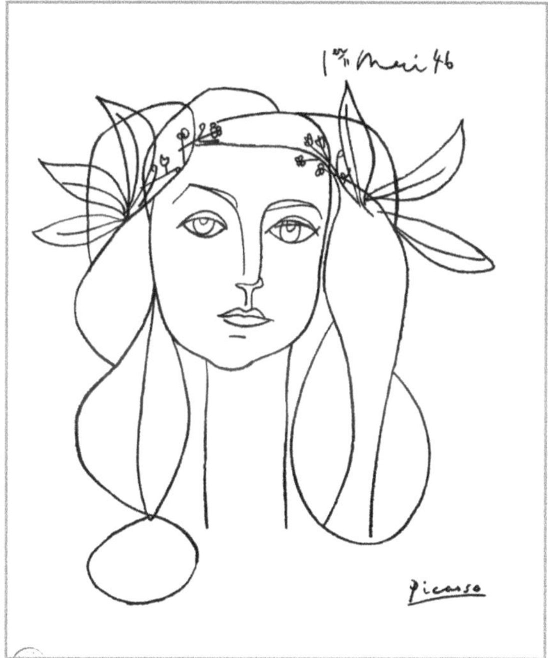

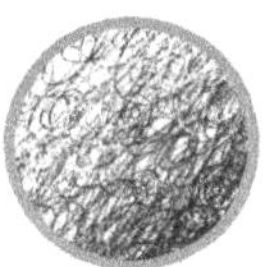 # Scribbling

Scribbling is a drawing method of creating tonal values by taking your pencil and continuously creating circles to fill in an area. You can create a change in tone by iintensifying the scribbling or by increasing the pressure on your pencil . You can also use shapes other than circles like figures of eight, loops or any other shapes that you can do continuously with your pencil or pen.

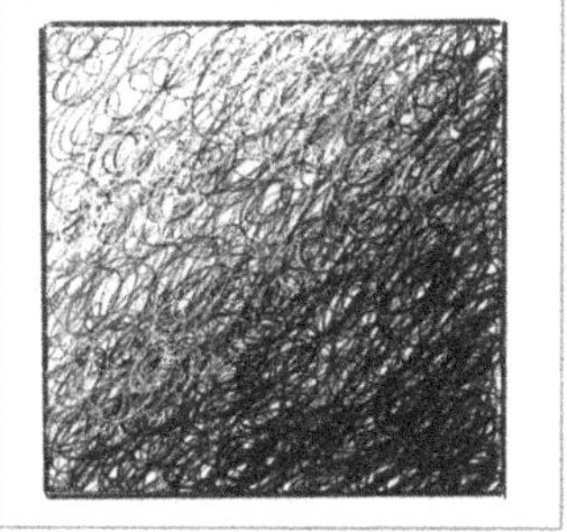

Scribbling exercises

1. Draw a square in your drawing book and fill it with circular scribbling.

2. Draw a second square and this time make your scribbling denser in one part and lighter in the other to create a graduated tone.

3. Draw a third square and this time alter the pressure you put on your pencil to create lighter and darker tones.

This drawing is by Alberto Giacometti, a famous sculptor and artist of the 20th century. Look how he creates the form of the face by scribbling lines as he sees them. I love this drawing technique and was very influenced by him when I was an art student many moons ago. I was uninspired by the way I was being taught to draw figures with neat lines and traditional shading techniques. It felt like a ' straitjacket' as it was all very predictable and boring.

"The more you fail, the more you succeed. It is only when everything is lost and - instead of giving up - you go on, that you experience the momentary prospect of some slight progress. Suddenly you have the feeling - be it an illusion or not - that something new has opened up."

Alberto Giacometti

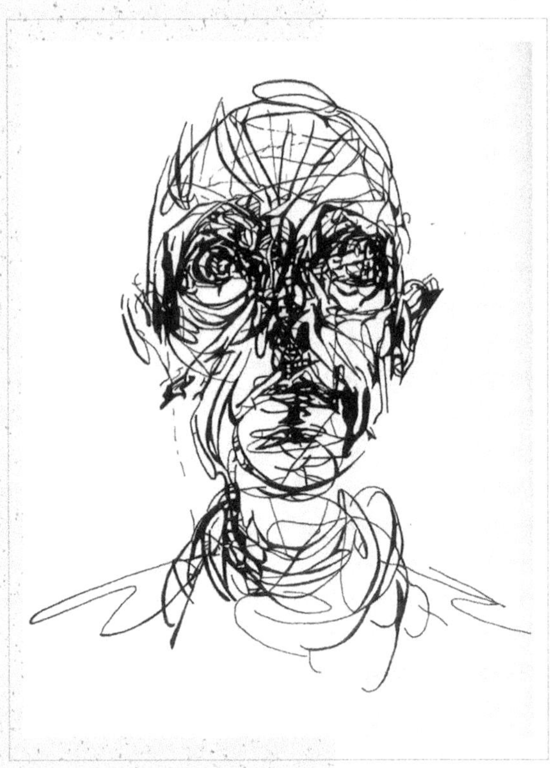

Alberto Giacometti
"Head" (1961)

What Giacometti has to say in this quote is vital to your success. You must be willing to fail and fail big when you start drawing. Do not give up just because you didn't succeed.

Of course this is a very personal thing, but you can see how drawing is an expression of your soul. There are no rights and wrongs, it is just how you feel about things and how you want to go about representing them.

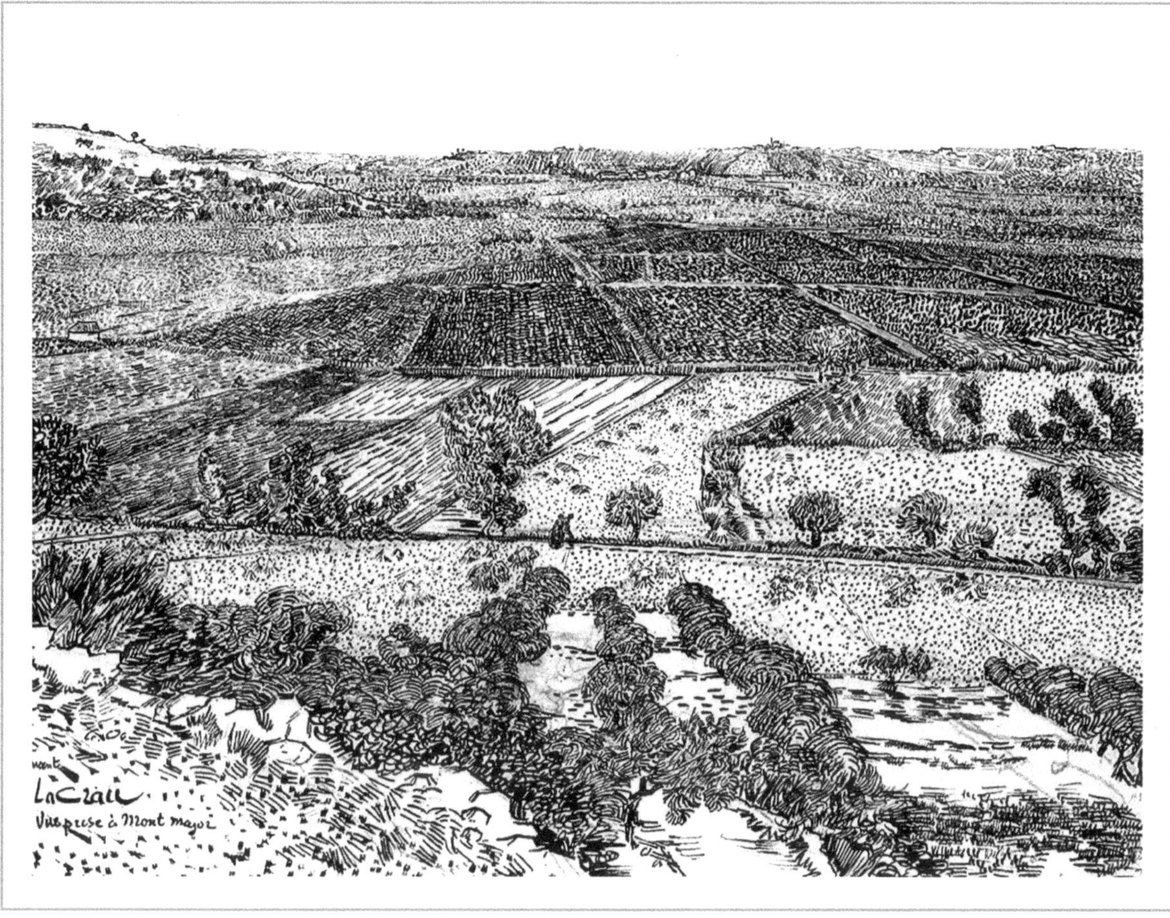

Vincent van Gogh
"La Crau Seen from
Montmajour" (1988)

Practicing everyday with these different drawing methods will help you create your own unique style of drawing.

As a final word on the matter I wanted to present to you one of the numerous drawings left behind by Vincent van Gogh.

Looking at it closely, you can see that he uses many of the methods and marks laid out in this chapter. He uses these different marks to describes the patterns he sees in nature and thus communicates the character of each surface, stippling dots for one field and hatched lines in different directions and so forth. This is one of my favorite drawings of all time!

FINAL EXERCISE: Scavenger Hunt

The final exercise in this chapter we have called SCAVENGER HUNT. Here's how it goes.

Walk around indoors and outdoors and pick up some different objects you find; some good examples are leaves, grasses, a piece of wood or bark or anything that has an interesting texture.

Your assignment is to execute at least three small sketches of whatever you find. You should select a different mark for each sketch.

You can select three (or more) different leaves, pieces of grass, acorns or whatever you found on your scavenger hunt and use a different mark for each one.

Alternately, you can use three different marks to draw the same thing.

Another suggestion that will make this easier is to draw a series of boxes about 3 inches square on your sketchbook or drawing pad, and then use this for your drawing. Experience shows this makes it easier to get started. Just fill the box!

On the opposite page we have shown you examples of the kind of things you might find on your scavenger hunt. You can always use these or take photographs, but best is to use the actual thing itself if possible.

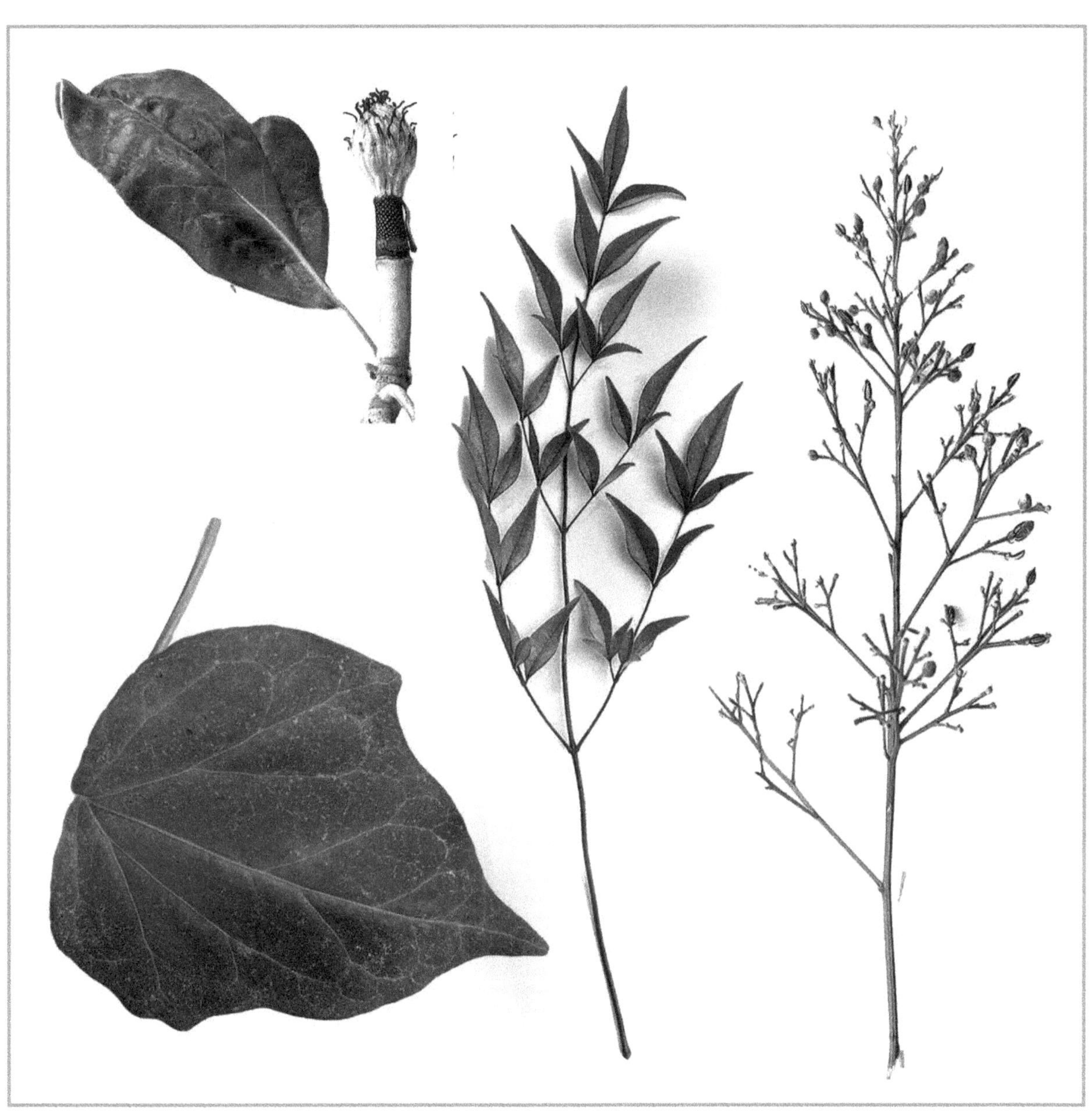

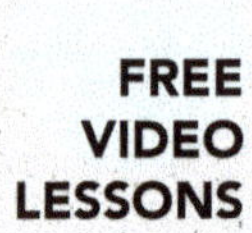

FREE VIDEO LESSONS

Traditional Drawing Video Demonstrations

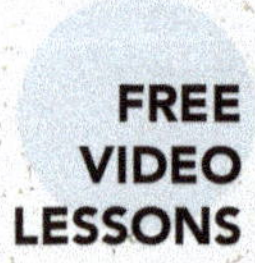

FREE VIDEO LESSONS

Digital Drawing Video Demonstrations

FREE WORKBOOK DOWNLOAD

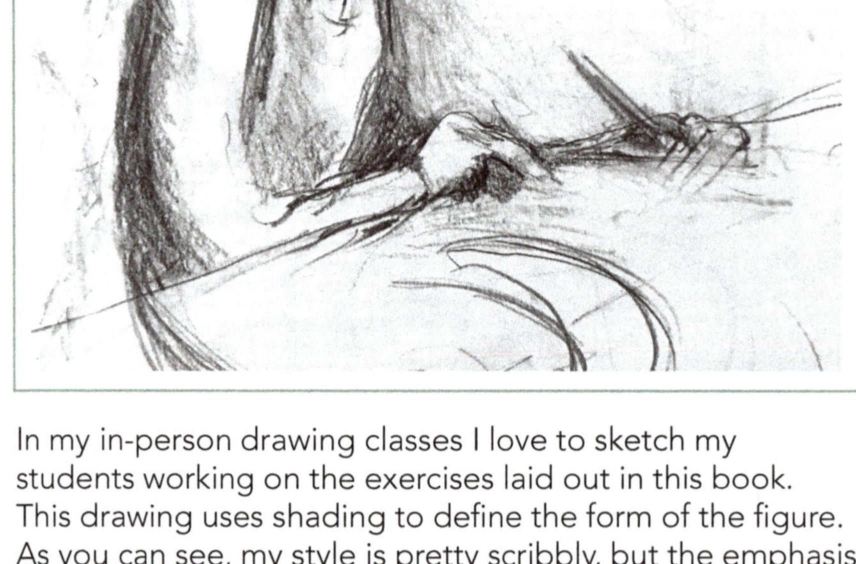

In my in-person drawing classes I love to sketch my students working on the exercises laid out in this book. This drawing uses shading to define the form of the figure. As you can see, my style is pretty scribbly, but the emphasis is on capturing the feeling I get from the figure.

Chapter 3: Shading and Shadows

A simple way to visualize tonal values is to take a photo on your smartphone, go to edit mode, turn it into a black and white photo. Now you can see that the light is represented by white, while shadows (or lack of light) are represented by black. Everything else is in between.

In this lesson we are going to learn to use shading techniques to represent tonal values, and that by doing this the drawing will become three-dimensional, even though you are drawing on a two-dimensional surface.

> "All the visible world is only light on form."
> Andrew Loomis

EXERCISE 1
Shading Practice

The first step is to learn to create a series of boxes as shown in the illustration, graduating from white to black or vice versa.

Take out your drawing pad and create a series of 8 boxes. You can use a ruler or just draw your own straight lines. It will look like the boxes pictured above.

Hold the pencil so the graphite is flat against the paper to create light shading strokes.

1. Take your 2B pencil and sharpen it so you have a large area of graphite. You will get a better result if you use a knife to sharpen rather than a pencil sharpener.

2. Turn the pencil on its side as shown, and very lightly cover the entire rectangle with a series of vertical lines. Remember to be VERY light. You will see why later.

3. Repeat this sequence, skipping the first box to be consistent.

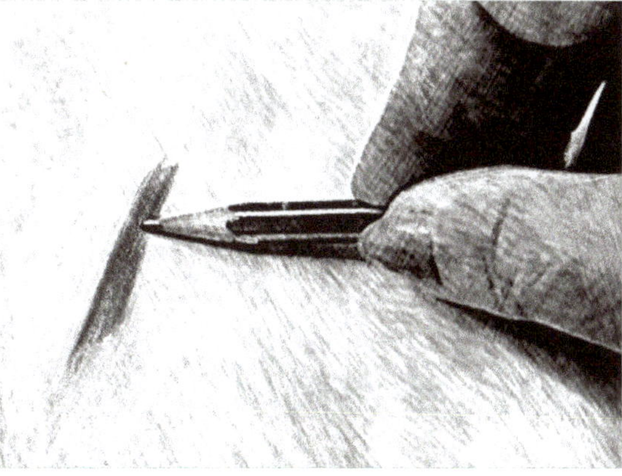

AHA!

Less is best! The lighter the marks, the more control you have. It's much easier to add more graphite than to erase it!

4. Repeat until all the boxes are filled, skipping a box each time.

When you are done you will note that you have a graduated set of boxes that go from light to dark.

Take your tortillon, hold it on its side so the flat edge of the tip is touching the paper.

Blend the marks in the box, noting that the tortillon not only smoothes out the lines, but also makes the shade somewhat darker.

If you went TOO dark, you can fix it by taking your kneaded eraser and using it to lift off excess graphite by "blotting" or stamping the area with the eraser.

The lighter your marks, the greater control you have. I recommend this light touch for your drawing until you have a good grasp of technique. Then with certainty, you can make dark lines without worrying if they are in the right place.

EXERCISE 2:
Tracing

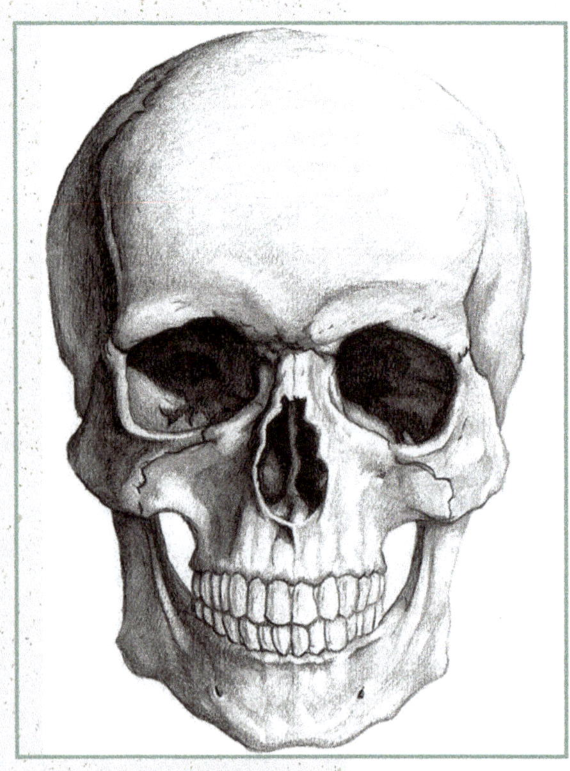

It is hard to erase, easy to add!

In this exercise you will be executing a perfect copy of this skull drawing to learn the technique of shading and see how tonal values help to create three dimensional form.

The first step is to trace the image so you can transfer it onto your drawing paper. Tracing is an age-old technique used by artists to copy an image. It is a basic learning tool, but more importantly a much needed step on this journey of drawing; it gives you guidelines that show you to where to put things. Tracing the image at this early stage of learning will give you the confidence to advance to the next stage.

I had one of my own "AHA!" moments when I attended a wonderful exhibition at the Asian Art Museum in San Francisco called 'East

Meets West'. In this exhibition I learned about the tremendous influence Japanese wood cuts had on some of my favorite 19th century impressionist and post impressionist painters. The artists collected Japanese prints and often produced their own graphic works that were directly inspired by the Japanese woodcuts that has been imported to Europe

by Far East traders.

One such artist was Vincent Van Gogh, a huge admirer and collector of these woodcuts. In the exhibition they displayed one of his carefully done tracings of one of his favorite Japanese prints.

Through research I learned that tracing was the way Van Gogh mastered drawing. He was self-taught and he used this technique to learn from other artists. You can see on

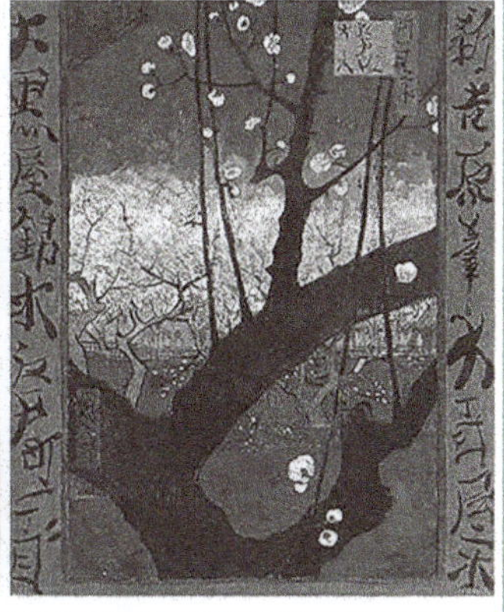

(Left: Hiroshige Plum Park in Kameido (1857)
Right: Vincent Van Gogh
"Flowering Plum) 1887

the right one of his tracings of an original Japanese woodcut which he greatly admired.

I recalled that, as a youngster in England, I would spend many hours tracing from my favorite books, copying illustrations of Winnie the Pooh, Peter Rabbit and other characters, with practice I could dispense with the tracing and copy it directly. Both techniques helped me master the skill of drawing at a young age.

Tracing the image

1. Place the skull image on your drawing board or a clean smooth surface.

2. Tear off a small amount of masking tape and tape the top down to hold it in place.

3. Tear off some tracing paper and place it over top of the image.

4. Attach it at the top with some tape so it doesn't move around when you are tracing!

5. Take your HB pencil and trace around each line of this image

PREPARING YOUR IMAGE

Use the QR code at the start of this chapter to access the free printable workbook. Use the link in Chapter 3 of the workbook to access this photo, download and print it.

6. Lift the tracing paper up from time to time to check you didn't forget any of the lines.

7. When you are done, remove the tape from both the image and tracing paper.

Transferring the image onto drawing paper

You will notice that the right and left sides of the original skull drawing are not identical. This means that you cannot simply turn your tracing over and transfer it onto the drawing page as it will come out in reverse.

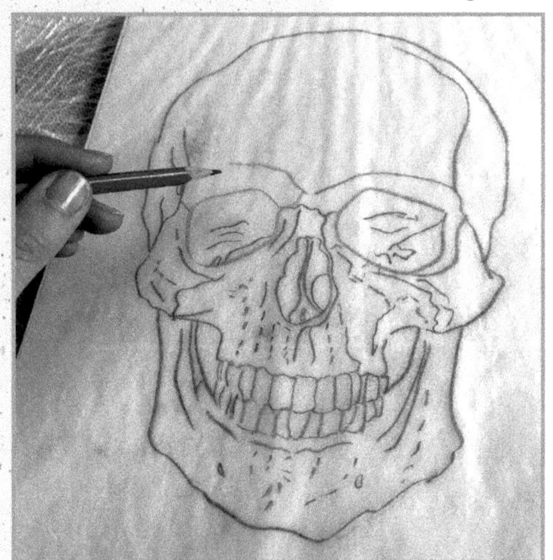

The solution is to turn the tracing over so the tracing is face down, and retrace it on the backside. Make sure to place the tracing paper on a piece of scrap paper before you start.

Use a 6B pencil to draw on the back of the tracing, following all the lines you can see through the tracing paper. This will give you a nice covering of graphite that you will use to transfer the image onto your drawing paper.

Once you are finished, turn the tracing paper over so the original tracing you did is now face up.

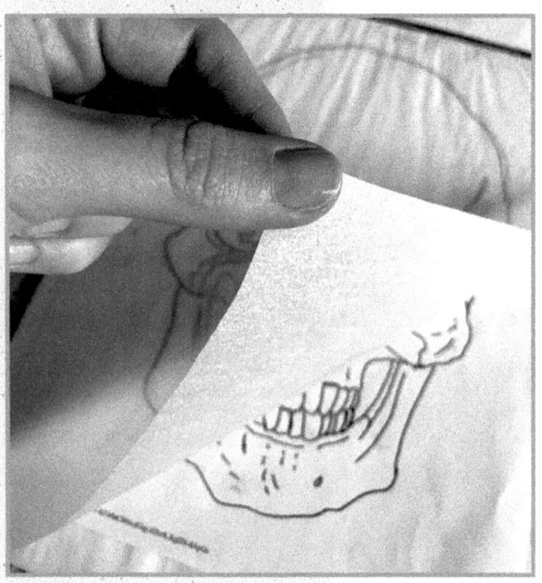

Place the tracing paper onto your drawing paper in the place you select for the drawing with the original tracing face upwards. Secure it in place with a strip of masking tape so the tracing paper doesn't move around.

Using the hardest pencil you have (2H if you have it), carefully draw over the whole tracing so you are transferring the black graphite pencil on the back of the tracing onto your drawing paper. You can check on your progress by lifting the tracing paper from time to time.

Once done, you will have lightly traced marks of the outlines of the skull that you will use as a guide for your drawing. You can now remove the tracing.

EXERCISE 3
Finishing

You will need your 2B and 6B pencils, your eraser, kneaded eraser and your tortillons, plus the original image of the skull for reference. Get set up on your table and ensure that the table top is smooth. You do not need to tape the paper down as you may want to move it around.

The first thing to remember is to start LIGHTLY. Do not just fill in all the dark parts as you will regret it later as we learned earlier in this lesson.

Start out shading at the top left of your drawing. By moving down the page you will avoid smudging the graphite by having to draw over the top of it. You can also move the paper around to avoid touching already drawn areas or use another piece of scrap paper to shield the marks you have already completed.

Using a 2B or softer pencil, start laying down the shading in the same way you did on your first exercise. Take your tortillon and blend the graphite. In this way you can easily blend the graphite from dark to light.

Now move through the whole drawing in this method. Gradually build up each area so it matches the tones in the original artwork.

Use your kneaded eraser when you need to remove some graphite, and use your hard eraser if you want to completely erase the graphite to create a highlight.

Do not rush this exercise, take your time. Put on some music and enjoy the journey.

Drawing is very meditative. Stay in the moment as you go through and complete each area.

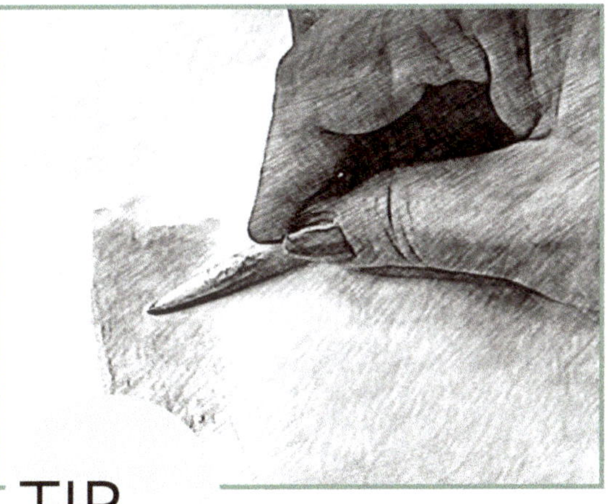

TIP

You will find that your tortillon will become black when you smudge the graphite. You can now use the tortillon loaded with graphite to shade in light areas on the top of the skull.

Try it out!

On the opposite page are some inspirational images to use to adorn your skull. You can find more by entering the name of whatever you want into a search engine, tapping images and saving the ones you like to your photo app.

Clean up your drawing.

When you are done, clean up the drawing by erasing any smudges from the white areas.

Show your family and friends, I am sure they will be super impressed. More importantly, you have learned the value of tonal shading, and you have experienced first hand how effective it is in creating a 3D object on a two-dimensional surface!!!

Protect your Image

Use a fixative spray to protect your drawing from smudging. If you don't have anything else, try some hair spray.

Once the drawing has been sprayed, the graphite underneath will not erase, it is fixed. Use proper ventilation as fixative stinks and is a potential hazard to your health, so consider spraying your drawing outside. Shake the can before spraying and test it on a scrap piece of paper, away from your drawing. Be careful the can doesn't spit and follow the

FINAL EXERCISE

instructions carefully on the fixative. Let it dry. You can draw on top of it if you need to.

You can leave your drawing at that if you like, however we suggest you take it a step further to insert your own creativity to the art.

You can add things to your drawing to create your own unique artwork. You can add flowers, snakes, dragons, a hat or some horns! Try printing off some images from the web. Then use the tracing technique to transfer them onto your drawing, checking they work size wise. Use some different mediums like colored pencils or markers. Anything goes! This is creativity time and there are no rules.

Once you are done, share your creation with your friends on social media and don't forget to tag us on our Instagram page @joyofdrawing .

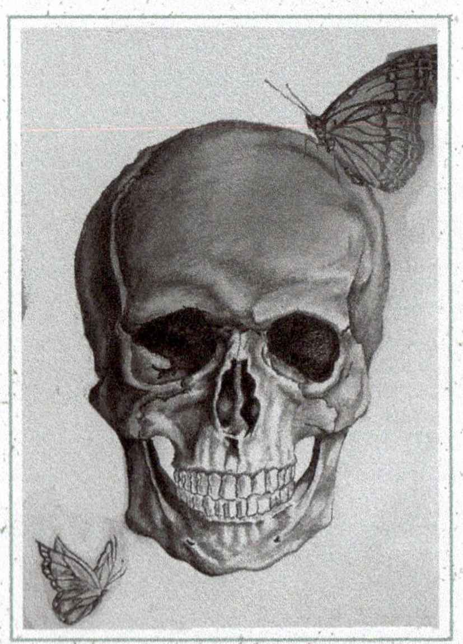

Decorated skull by a Joy of Drawing beginning student

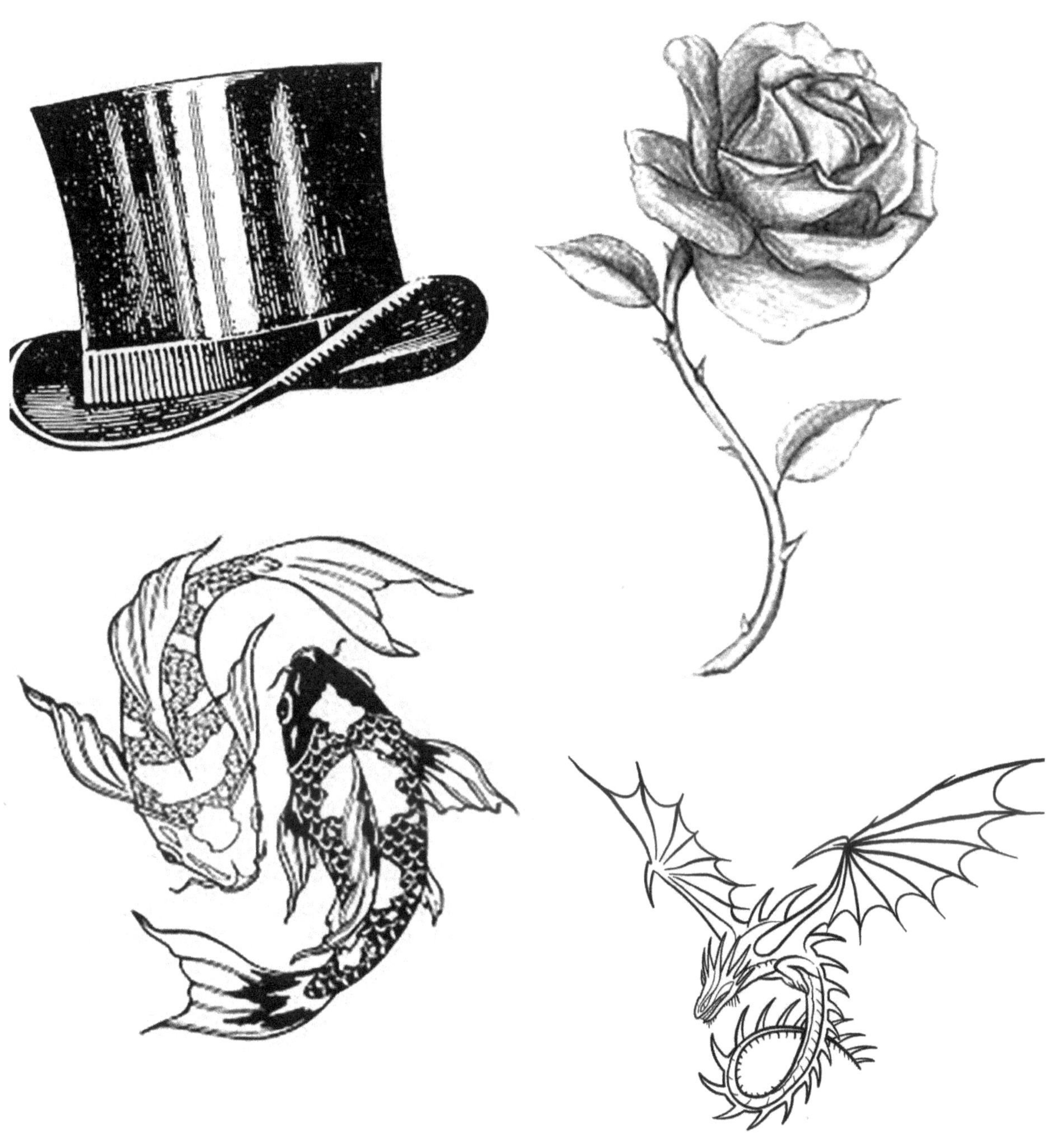

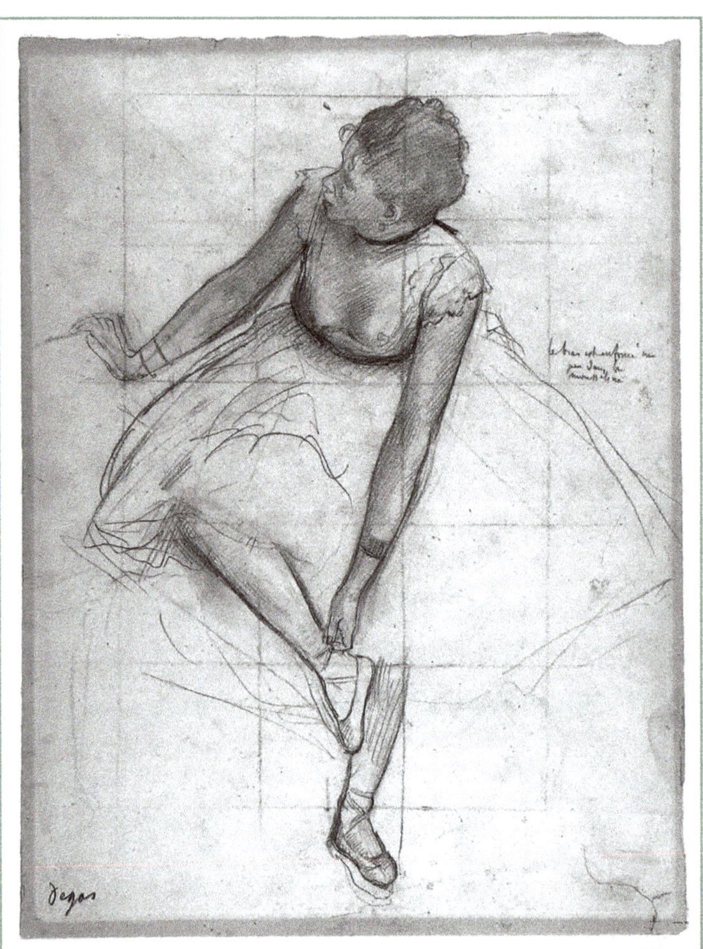

Edgar Degas "Dancer Adjusting Her Slipper" (1973)

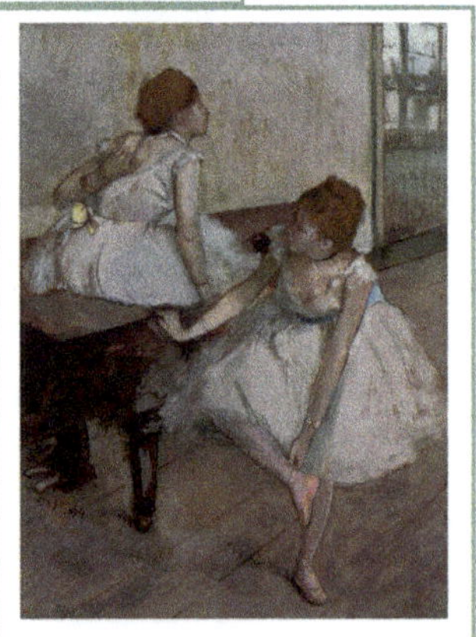

Edgar Degas "Twp Dancers Resting" (1974)

In this drawing by Edgar Degas you can see lines criss crossing the drawing. As you will learn in this chapter, these are called grid lines and one of their uses is to transfer a drawing to another artwork. Degas used these lines to transfer the drawing to the pastel shown on the right.

Chapter 4: Gridding

Have you ever wondered how mural artists create perfect renditions of their subject matter on such a huge surface? From the earliest mural painters in the Renaissance to the present day, the answer is the use of a technique called gridding.

With the tracing technique, you can only transfer an image of the exact same size. With gridding you can go from the original to any size, larger or smaller.

This is the next step on your journey, and teaches you some very important skills.

You will begin to appreciate and notice that successful drawing is about the RELATIONSHIP of one thing to another.

EXERCISE 1
Gridding Practice

This illustration shows a hand with a grid drawn over it and another grid underneath it. Use the QR code on the opposite page and print the image using the link provided in Chapter 4 of the workbook.

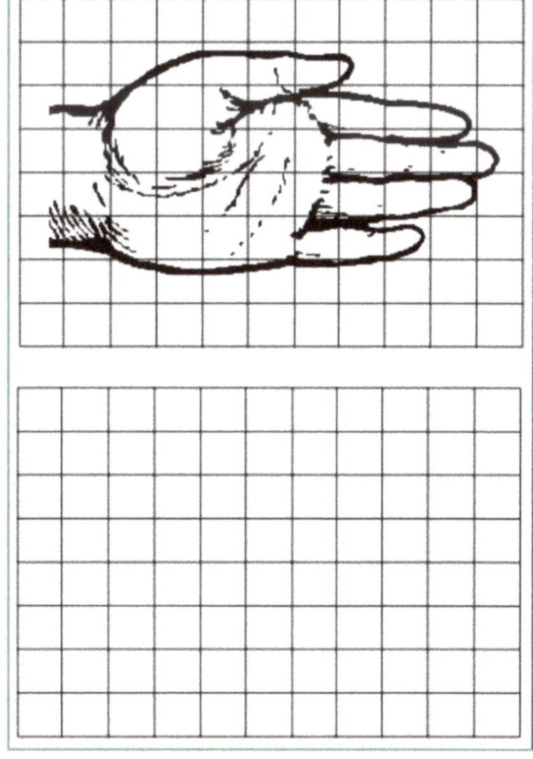

Take it slowly and copy the hand onto the lower grid. Start at the left and mark where each of the lines intersect each square. Do not try to draw a hand. Instead, draw each line as you see it in the corresponding square in the top drawing. That way you will end up with a perfectly drawn hand that exactly matches the drawing at the top.

TIP! Try turning the page upside down so you are not distracted by the fact it is a hand but just concentrate on the lines and shapes.

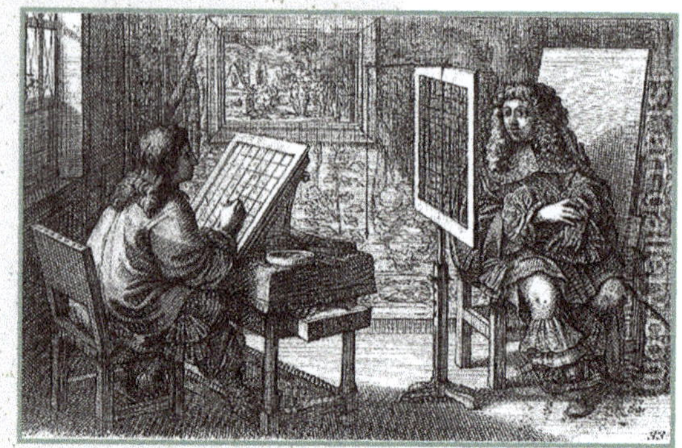

Gridding was also used by artists to ensure their portraits were accurate. They would place a finely gridded screen between themselves and their subject as seen in this illustration. They would then draw or paint on paper or canvas covered in a grid matching the number of squares in the screen.

EXERCISE 2
Using a grid to copy an image

Step One: Select an image to draw

The first step is to select something you would like to draw. Here are the things to check before you finalize your choice:

- **Is the image large enough?** You can of course find images on a search engine, but many are very small (1 x 2 inches) and too small for this exercise. You can overcome this by putting *hi res* (high resolution) or *large* at the end of your search item.

- **Good contrast:** Make sure the photo you select has good contrast with clear black and whites and midtones. This is an important factor. This might be hard to see in a colored photo, so the next step is vital in terms of finalizing your image.

- **Make the image black and white:** You can do this very rapidly on your phone by selecting edit and selecting black and white. Then you can see if the image has good enough contrast.

- **Finally, choose something you really want to draw:** This is important because, if you really want something you will take the time to create it. This exercise can take a while so spend your time drawing an image you love and it will worth the time and effort you put into it!

Use the link provided in Section 4 of the workbook to download and print the photo of the cat used in the remaining exercises in this chapter. If you are using an iPad you can download it to your photos using the link provided in Section 4.

Step Two: Create your grid

Now you have your photo, print TWO copies on 8 1/2 x 11 paper. You can use photo paper for one and regular paper for the other. Or regular for both.

Now you are going to draw a grid all over the print on regular paper. For this you need a fine tip black pen and a ruler.

1. First of all measure the exact size of the image (not the paper). Write down length and width.

2. Next divide each measurement in half.

3. Take the short side of the image and mark the half way point on the top and bottom of the image.

4. Do the same for the long side of the image.

5. Use your ruler to connect the dots together. You will have a line that divides the image in half.

6. Now do the same on the longer side of the image. Mark the halfway point each side. Use your ruler to connect the dots.

7. Next is to mark off one inch dots starting at the center point of the longer side of the image to the edge, then the same to the other edge.

8. Repeat these steps for the shorter side, again starting at the middle and working outwards.

9. Use these dots to rule lines horizontally, each one inch apart crisscrossing the shorter side of the image.

10. You will find that the image will probably end in the middle of a square on the sides. That is fine.

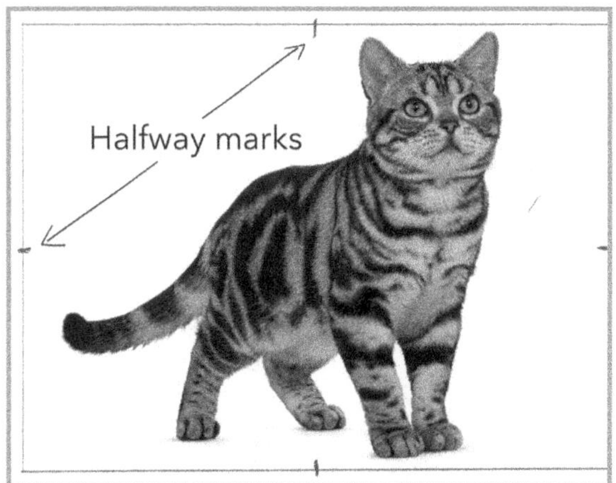

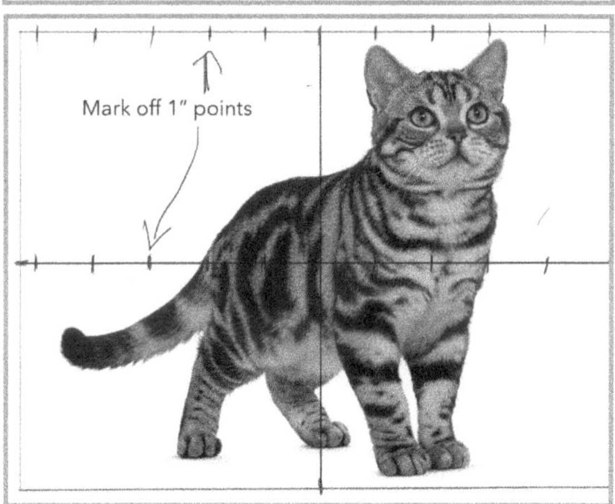

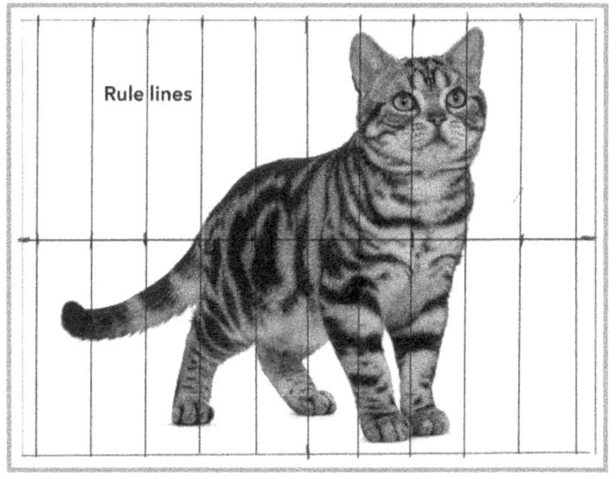

AHA!

Don't underestimate the importance of this part of the journey. You are learning to notice RELATIONSHIPS— the cornerstone of being able to draw.

Later in this book you will learn how to do this without the need of tracing or grid lines, but for now enjoy the results of your hard work and carry on!

Alternate method: You can also purchase a transparent sleeve and, using your pen and ruler, repeat the above exercise drawing the grid directly on the front of the sleeve. Once done, you can place any photo or drawing inside the sleeve and the grid will show over top of it. Once done you can remove your image intact.

Step Three: Prepare your drawing paper

Take your drawing paper, hopefully larger than the size of the paper with your image. This will give you the best experience of this method. You will be drawing the same image but larger than original.

You must now work out the size of the squares on the larger sized paper. Here are the steps:

1. Firstly, count the number of squares on the shorter side of your image. It must be a round number. For example in the cat photo the number is 8.

2. Next, measure the shorter side of your drawing paper.

3. Divide the number of squares into the size of the paper you just measured. The result will be a number. Use that number to measure out the size of the squares on you are now going to draw on your paper.

4. Now it is time to create those squares.

5. Take an HB pencil and your ruler.

6. Mark off the halfway points each side of the paper and connect them so you have a cross in the middle of the paper.

7. Starting at the middle of the longest middle line, measure off squares using the number you arrived at in step 3 above.

8. Repeat this for the shorter middle line.

9. Repeat the above on the edges of the paper, always starting your marking at the middle line on the page.

10. Rule all the lines, connecting the dots so you have a grid which crisscrosses your drawing paper.

NOTE: You may have more boxes on the long side of the

paper as the paper proportion might be different from your printer paper. This is not a problem.

Step Four: Draw in the outlines

Following the same procedure you took in copying the hand, draw in the outlines of the image, square by square Remember, you are not drawing the object, you are copying each square getting the exact points where lines intersect and the shape of the lines within each square. You must be very observant and meticulously move from one square to the next. Pretty soon you will have an accurate outline!

Next is to draw in key features such as eyes, nose, mouth, chin and so forth.

Next is to draw in anything you know you will need such as the shapes of markings or shadows and so forth.

Take stock of your progress. When you feel you have accurately drawn in the main points of your image, you can now erase the grid and dispense with the gridded copy of your image.

Step Five: Complete your drawing

Take the second copy of your image without the grid lines, and use it as your reference to complete your drawing, You can use the same method you used in the previous chapter to shade in your drawing, or you can use one or more of the different texturing techniques. Finish your drawing until you are really proud and happy with the results.

Once you are done you can repeat the whole gridding process with a photo of your own choice!

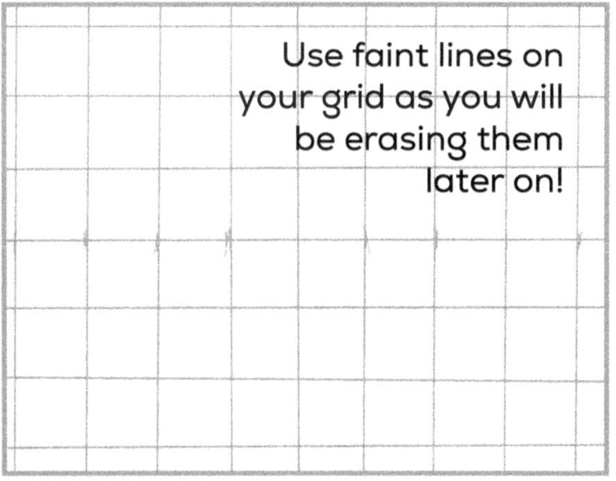

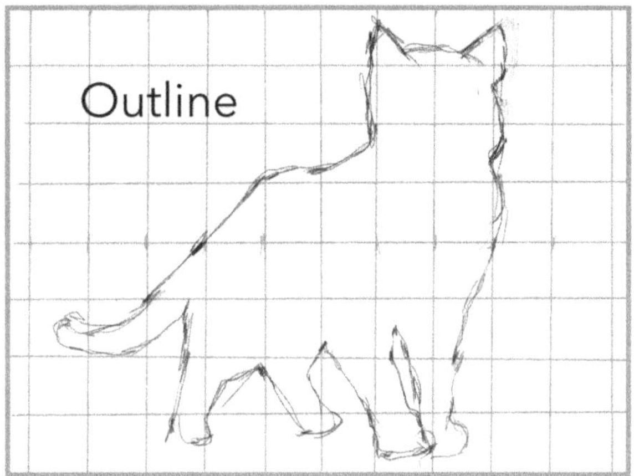

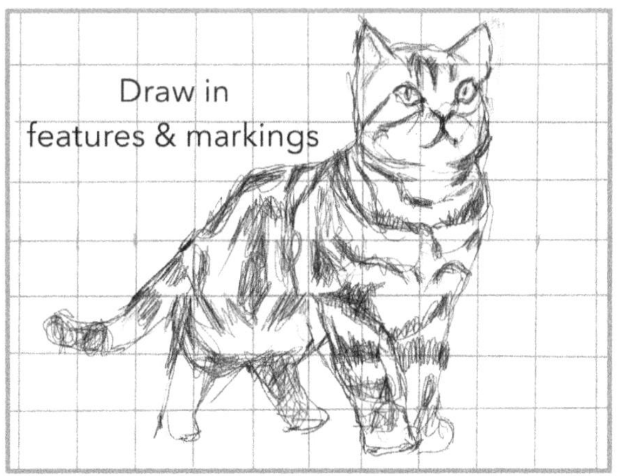

Sketch in the outline first and then fill in important details. Erase the grid when done.

FREE VIDEO LESSONS

Traditional Drawing Video Demonstrations

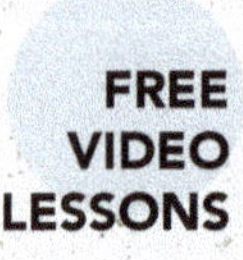

FREE VIDEO LESSONS

Digital Drawing Video Demonstrations

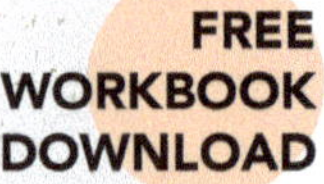

FREE WORKBOOK DOWNLOAD

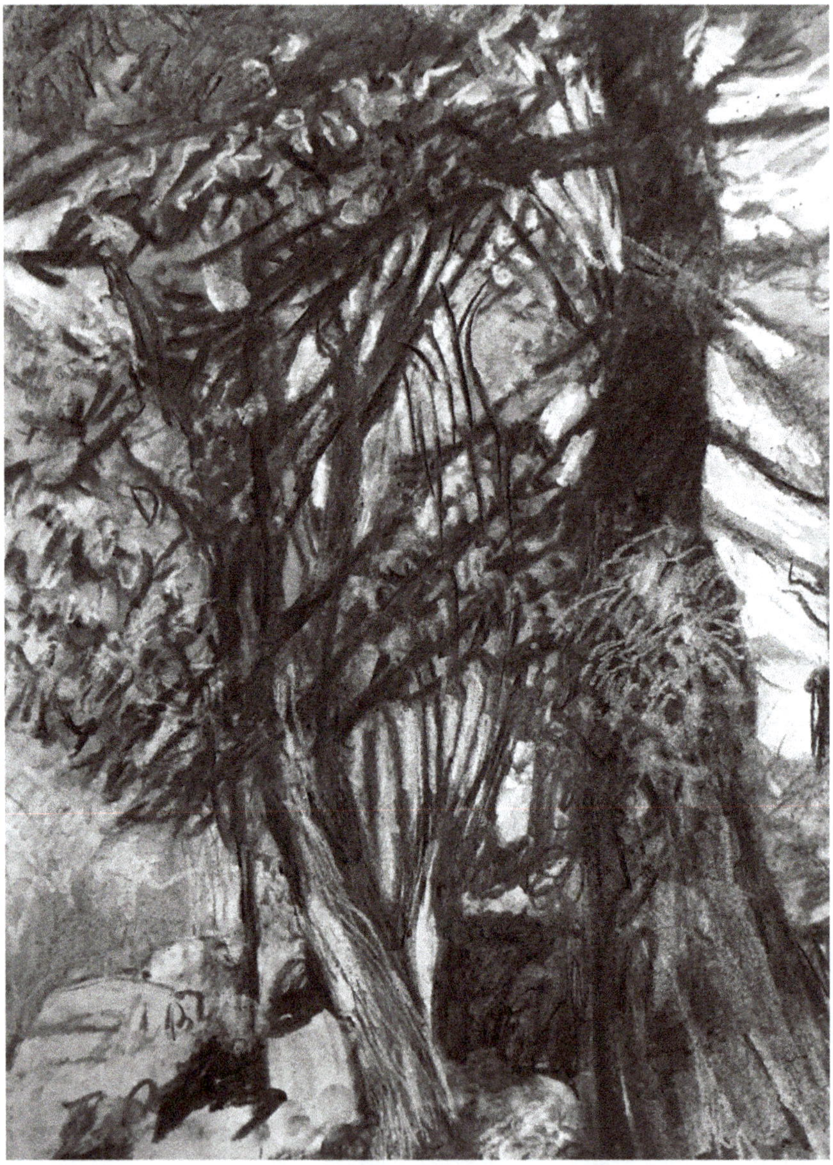

This large charcoal was created looking out the window at the trees on the corner of Forest and Ramona in Palo Alto. I love the expressive quality of this medium, and the speed with which one can work.

Chapter 5: Charcoal

In Chapters 3 and 4 we required you to have a deep concentration and careful adherence to shading rules. These techniques tend to satisfy the more detail-oriented souls amongst us. However, in this lesson we are going to break free and explore a different side of drawing.

Set yourself up on a covered table as the lessons in this chapter will be MESSY! Put on an old shirt or a pinafore (as we say in the UK). Protect your clothes and expect to make your hands dirty so have some wipes or paper towels nearby.

You're going to get messy because in this lesson, instead of your pencil you will be using charcoal.

A word here about the difference between charcoal and graphite which, up to this point, you have been using. While both come from carbon, the way they are made creates two distinctive drawing techniques.

Graphite is best for the kind of detailed work we did in the last two lessons.

Charcoal is used to create expressive and dramatic marks and preliminary rapid sketches. There is a sense of freedom when you make marks with charcoal that you will experience in this lesson.

> "All art is dependent on technology because it's a human endeavor, so even when you're using charcoal on a wall or designing the proscenium arch, that's technology."
> George Lucas

EXERCISE 1
Learn how to use charcoal

Get yourself set up with some rough paper or newsprint if you have it. Pick up a medium sized piece of charcoal.

STAND UP IF YOU CAN - this allows you to make big sweeping gestures when you draw and will give you better control.

Move your shoulder or your elbow around to create sweeping, expressive lines and marks.

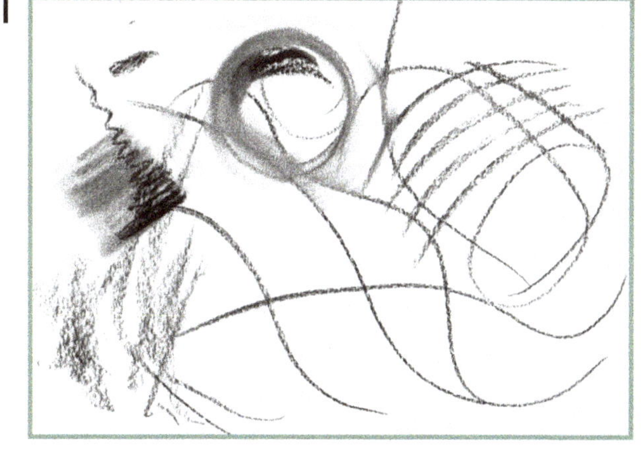

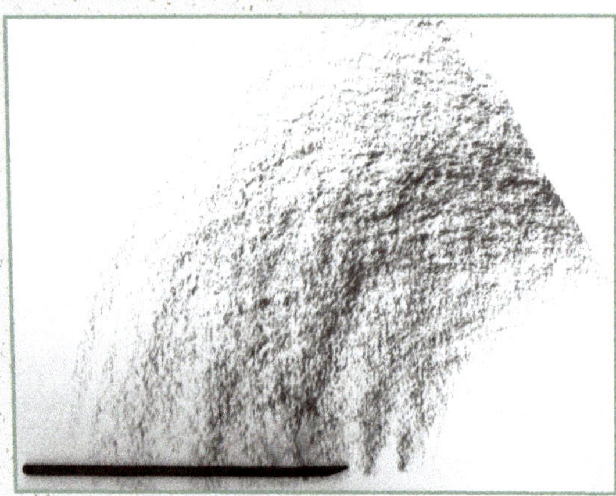

 **Place the charcoal on its side and swipe it across the paper to create a large patch of shading.**

Using the overhand grip, hold the charcoal so the side of the stick connects to the paper and drag it over the paper to create large patches of charcoal.

Try using your fingers to rub the charcoal around and smudge to create different types of textures.

Use your kneaded eraser to erase through the charcoal and expose the white paper underneath.

Doodle as much as you like to experiment with different sizes of charcoal, different amounts of pressure and so forth.

Some people experience an immediate dislike of this medium, and if that is you, keep going and try to stick it out. If you like you can replace the charcoal with a large stick of graphite or with a conté crayon.

EXERCISE 2
Drawing with charcoal

Take out the black and white photo from Chapter 4 to use as a guide. You are already familiar with it in terms of where the shadows go and so forth.

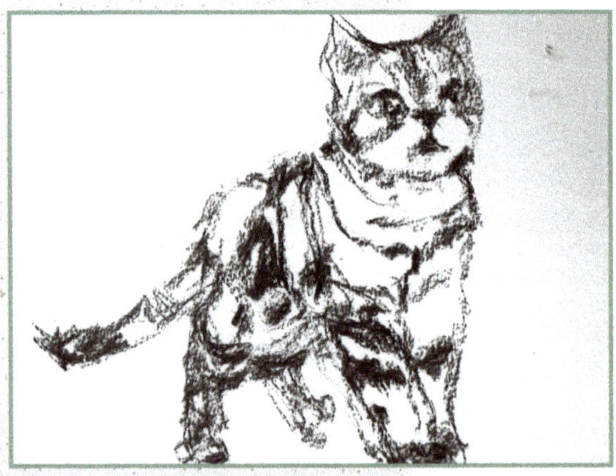

Layout a large piece of paper and use the charcoal to draw in the shadows expressively without worrying about small details.

The challenge is to loosen up; do not concern yourself with being precise. Trust your instincts and accept that it won't be perfect — but it will have a charm all of its own.

Use your fingers to smudge the charcoal and use your kneaded eraser to wipe off excess or to reveal a highlight.

Experiment with your hard eraser for the best result.

EXERCISE 3
Drawing by Erasing

In this exercise, instead of using the charcoal to draw in the shadows, you are using the eraser to reveal the light!

Using the same photo, take a piece of paper and this time cover it with charcoal by placing the stick of charcoal on its side, cover the whole page with charcoal, crisscrossing back and forth. Once done, smudge it so the charcoal is evenly distributed across the page.

Take an eraser, use the photo as your guide, erase out the lighter areas of the photo to reveal the shapes of the object.

Notice what a contrasting but interesting effect it has, with practice this can be a useful tool to have in your drawing repertoire.

Sometimes you may want to make an area extra white. You can make highlights brighter by using white conté crayon.

Keep working the drawing until you are happy with it. Lay it beside the first drawing and notice the difference in character between the two techniques.

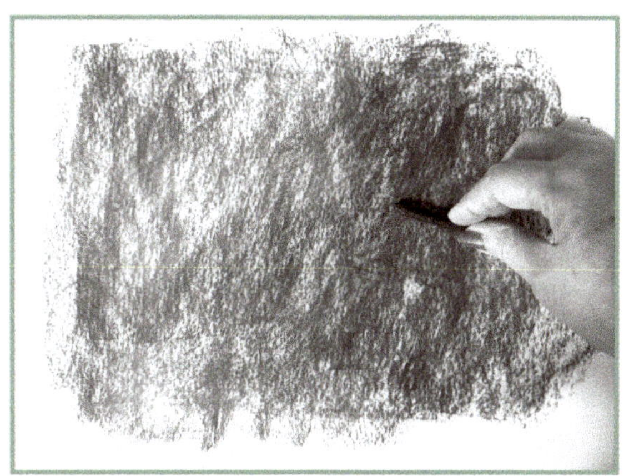

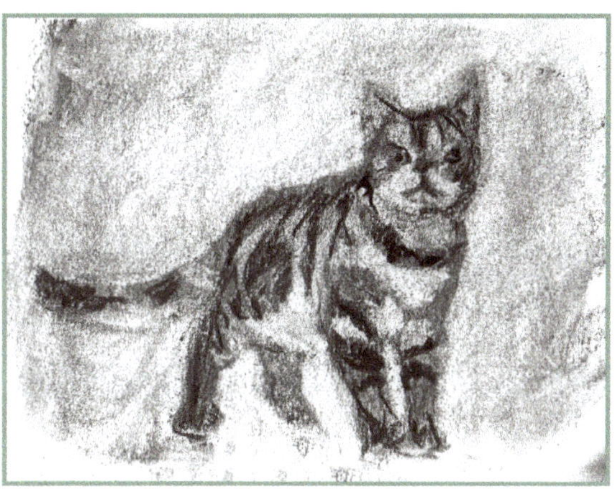

Cover the whole page with charcoal and use your eraser to remove charcoal and reveal the image!

FINAL EXERCISE

Select a new black and white photo that you have never copied before, lay it beside a fresh piece of charcoal paper and start again.

I am always amazed at how well these drawings turn out. I personally love charcoal although I went through a phase of hating the sensation of feeling it, and thus understand some people just cannot easily tolerate it. If that includes you, do not worry. Just find a replacement drawing tool to do this exercise such as conté and you will be fine!

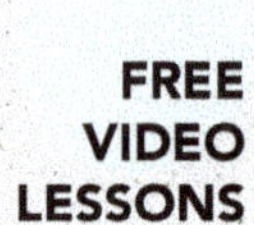

FREE VIDEO LESSONS

Traditional Drawing Video Demonstrations

FREE VIDEO LESSONS

Digital Drawing Video Demonstrations

FREE WORKBOOK DOWNLOAD

Wassily Kandinsky
"Analysis of Still Life"
(1929)

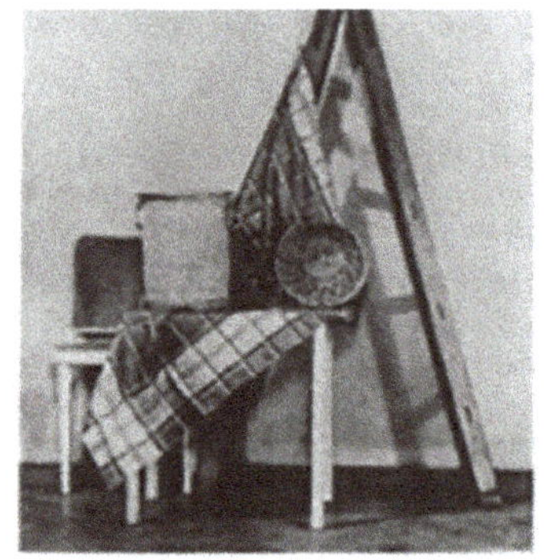

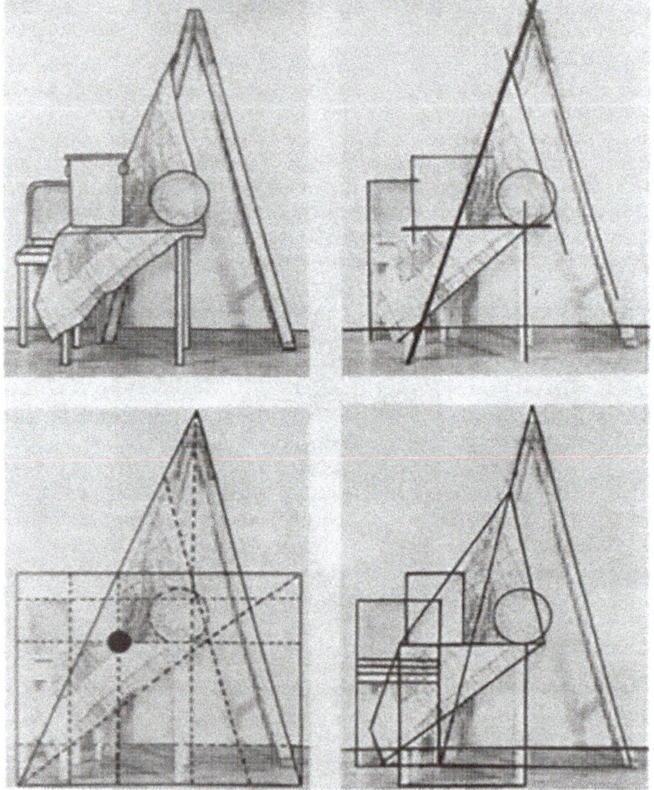

This illustration shows four drawings created by Wassily Kandinsky based on the photo of the still life at the top. It was drawn in 1929 as part of the analytical drawing class he delivered at the Bauhaus Art School in Germany. Here you can see how he simplifies what he sees in the still life shown in the photo to basic shapes and forms.

Chapter 6: Shapes & Forms

Now you have gained some basic drawing skills, it's time to take the first big step towards being able to draw without the need of any assistive tools such as tracing paper or grids. We call this "drawing without a net". Or just drawing what you see in front of you.

In the next three chapters you are going to learn to objectively analyze what you see and break it down into basic lines and shapes.

"The first things to study are form and values. For me, these are the things that are the basics of what is serious in art."

Jean Baptiste Corot

EXERCISE 1
Curved vs straight lines

In the first lesson we will observe the most fundamental types of lines and then look around for them in your immediate environment.

Curved lines can create different organic shapes such as those most frequently seen in nature. Look around the room and find some curved lines and draw what you see: Leaves on a plant, petals on a flower, fruit and flowing fabric.

There are three types of straight lines:

* Vertical lines that go straight up or down such as the sides of a door frame, a building or a telephone pole

* Horizontal lines such as the horizon on the ocean or the bottom of your TV screen

* Diagonal lines - any lines that are angled such as the sides of a mountain or one of the pyramids or the spokes on a bike wheel.

Look around the room to observe and identify the three types of straight lines. Make a

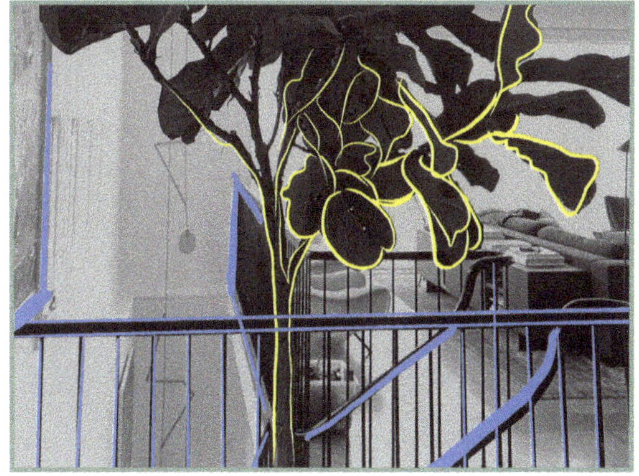

In this photo we identified each of the types of lines: curvy for the plant, vertical, horizontal and diagonal for the stair rails.

sketch of them if you like.

Already you have begun to analyze what you see and break it down what you see into curved or straight lines, including the further analysis of the straight lines as vertical, horizontal or diagonal. This step alone starts you on the road to easily notice what you are looking at.

Forget whether it is a door or a chair, a vase or a flower and simply analyze what you see in terms of type of lines that make up the scene.

EXERCISE 2
Primary & combination shapes

Translating what we observed about the basic types of lines, we can now start thinking about shapes.

There are three primary shapes that make up every other shape that exists. No, this is not a geometry lesson. It is simply a new way of looking at things. The more you can break down what you see into simple lines and shapes, the faster you will be able to represent them in your drawing.

Just as we can break down color into three primary colors that make up all the colors of the rainbow, so we can break down shapes. This was the core learning of The Bauhaus, the famous art school established in Germany in 1919, 100 years ago. The teaching at this school had huge influence on 20th century architecture, design and fine art. Some of the greatest artists of the earlier 20th century taught students attending the school until it was closed down by the Nazis in the mid 1930s.

The Square ■ The Circle ● The Triangle ▲

All man-made objects can be broken down into a combination of these three primary shapes.

Knowing that really helps us when we want to draw them! Even organic objects, including the human body, can be analyzed by breaking them down into these primary shapes.

The Square ■

Living in a house you will most likely see a lot of square or rectangular shapes as that is the basic building block of a home. Rugs, tablecloths, picture frames you name it. This shape is most prominent in any man made environment. We are including the rectangle in this as it is an extended square or two squares joined together.

The Circle ●

Starting with the moon and the sun and coming all the way down to the beach ball, the circle is the second obvious basic shape you see around you. We include the ellipse or oval as they are based on circle.

You will see many circles and ellipses exist as you look around - oranges and apples, hats and umbrellas, plates and jam jars. Lots and lots of circles and ellipses.

The Triangle ▲

Here is the last primary shape.   Any three straight lines con-nected at each end. That's a triangle.

Combination Shapes

● ▲When you mix a triangle with a circle you get a cone.

● ■ When you mix a circle with a square or rectangle, you get lots of interesting shapes as you can see in this illustration.

This exercise will help you see this in the surrounding room as demonstrated in this illustration.

Take the three primary shapes and observe them in your en-vironment. As we have done in this photo on page 51, try breaking down what you see around you in the room into cir-cles or ellipses, squares or rect-angles and triangle, or combi-nations of them.

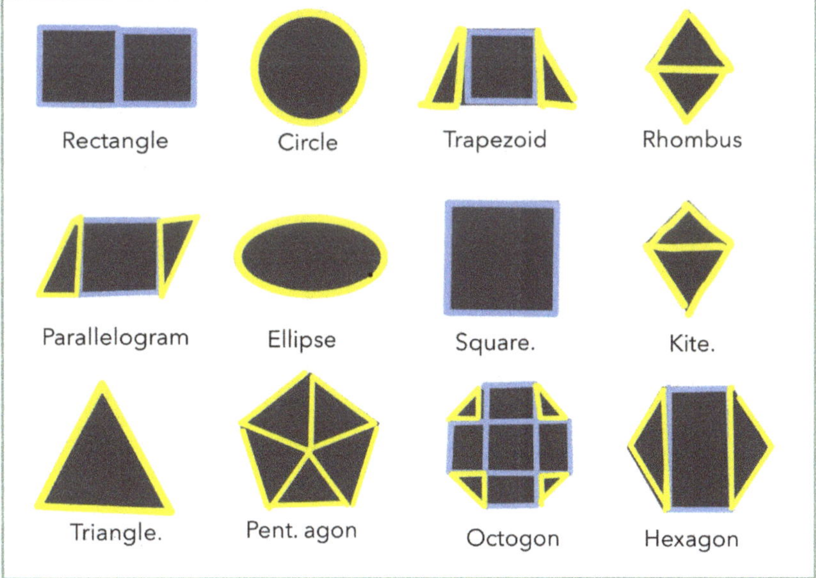

Each of these geometric figures are made from one or more of three primary shapes - the square, circle and triangle.

Again, forget you are looking at objects with names. Just view them as shapes. This simplification makes it much easier to describe what you see.

EXERCISE 2
Primary & combination forms

A form is a three dimensional version of a shape.

The Cube ■ The Sphere ● The Pyramid ▲

All three of these objects are based on a single shape. The sphere is based on the circle, the cube on the square and the pyramid on the triangle.

Next come forms which are a combination of two of the three primary forms

- A cone is a combination of a triangle and a circle

- A cylinder is a combination of a square or rectangle and a circle

- A four sided pyramid is a combination of a square base with four triangular sides.

Draw each of these shapes, starting with the three primary forms. We will begin by drawing them as outlines, and in the final exercise we will shade them in to make them appear three-dimensional.

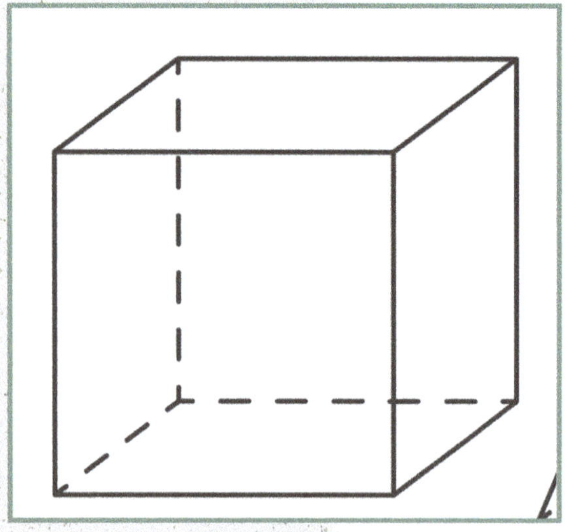

The Cube ■

We are not here attempting to teach you to use perspective in drawing your cube. Instead here is an easy way to draw a cube.

1. Draw a square and then draw a second square which is slightly higher up on the page and overlapping the first square.

2. Now connect the corners of the square to each other. Then erase what you do not need so you have what appears to be a solid cube. Voilá!

The Sphere ●

This is, of course, a circle. Until you add shading it is hard to make it appear to be a form. You may need to review how to draw an accurate circle by revisiting the exercise in Chapter One.

You can include the ellipse shapes to give the sphere depth as shown in this illustration.

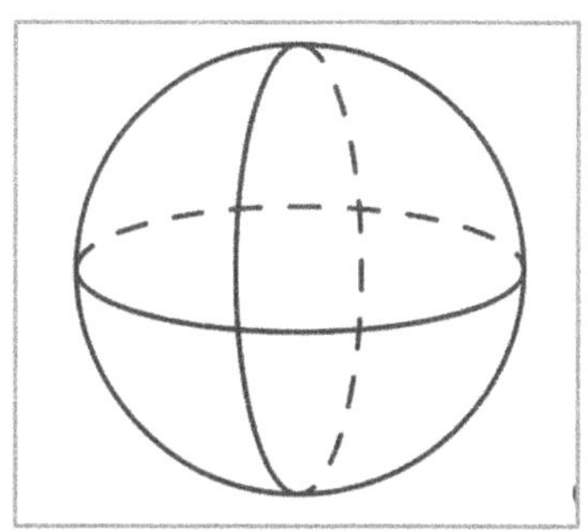

The Pyramid ▲

Draw a triangle and, like this illustration, notice you will not be able to see the back sides of the pyramid because they recede behind the triangle in front! So draw some more triangles so it looks like the illustration.

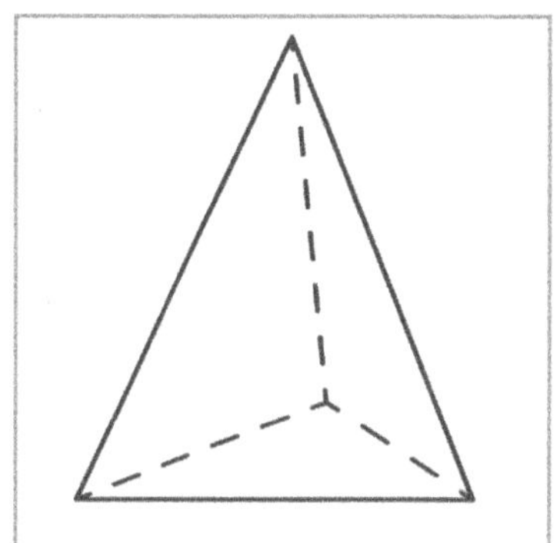

Combination forms

The remaining forms are combinations of the primary forms as you will see in the exercises connected to them.

The cone is a combination of a circle for the base and a triangle for the sides. Here's how to draw a cone:

1. Draw a straight vertical line, then draw a horizontal line crossing it.

2. Mark off your oval shape which will form the bottom of your cone and draw it as you did in the prior exercise.

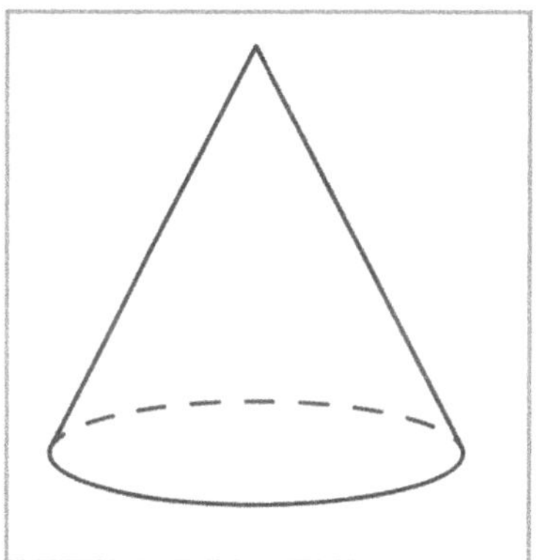

3. Now mark the top of the tone on the vertical line and connect to each edge of the oval. Erase what you no longer need.

The cylinder is a combination of straight lines and circle. Here's how to draw one.

1. Draw an ellipse. If you have trouble making it even, begin by drawing a straight horizontal like and crossing it with a vertical line. Now mark points equidistant from the center as shown. This will help you create a balanced oval shape. Again, use the technique used in creating the circle.

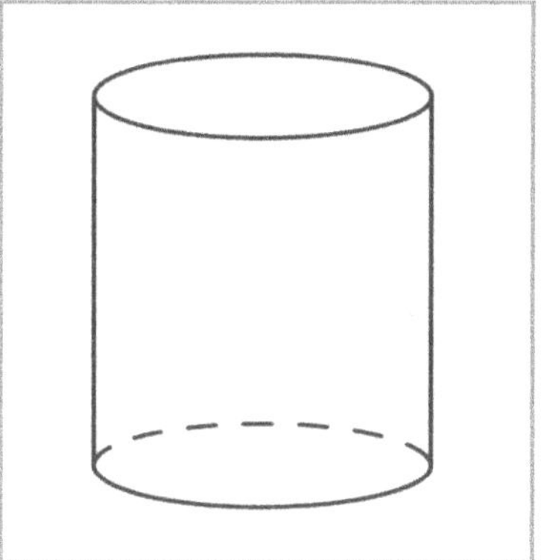

2. Now draw the vertical sides of the cylinder so they end at the same point and at the top repeat the same ellipse you created at the bottom.

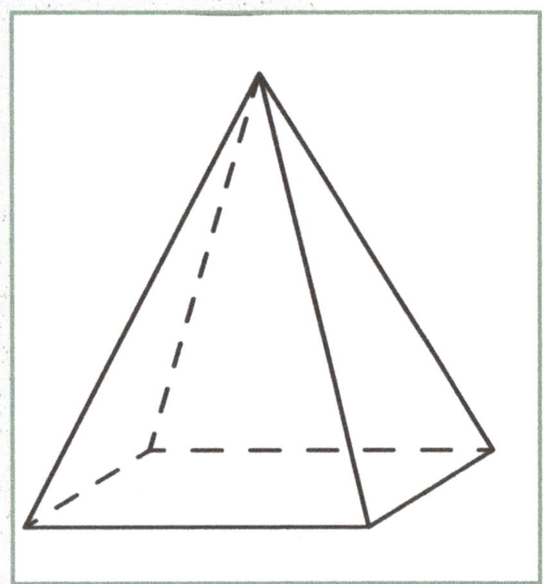

The four sided pyramid is a combination of triangles and a square base. Here's how to draw one:

1. Draw a straight line for the front of the pyramid and a shorter line for the back and connect the back to the front as shown.

2. Mark the middle of the front line and draw a vertical line. Mark off the top of the pyramid on the vertical line and connect it to each end of each of the two lines you drew for the base as shown in the illustration.

EXERCISE 2
Forms and values

Now we are going to make your drawings three dimensional using the shading techniques you mastered in Chapter Three.

In this lesson you are going to analyze where the shading should go based on the direction of the light hitting the object. We need light to illuminate the objects around us. Without it we only see darkness.

Leonardo da Vinci highlights this in the quote about light. He would begin by making his whole canvas black and then illuminated the objects so they became visible. This is much like the second charcoal drawing exercise you executed in the previous chapter.

The use of light and shadow makes it possible to represent things in three dimensions. Practicing drawing simple forms enables you to analyze where the light falls and thus which part of the object will be in shadow. It also teaches you to see the direction of the shadow it casts on the ground underneath it. And it transforms shapes into three dimensional objects.

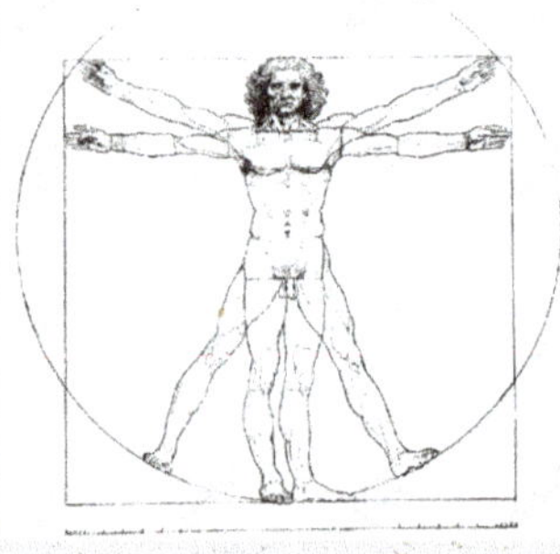

"A painter should begin every canvas with a wash of black, because all things in nature are dark except where exposed by the light."
Leonardo da Vinci

Let's begin with the cube

Depending on the direction of the light, it will illuminate the planes it hits directly. The planes that are hidden from the light will thus be black, and the planes where light can reach a little will be a mid tone.

The shape and direction of the shadow cast by the cube will depend on the position of the light. Like the midday sun, if the light is directly above the cube the shadow it casts will be very small. But, like the sun, as it moves lower and lower, the shadow grows longer and longer, just like the length of shadows when the sun is just rising or setting. And of course, the shadow will be in the opposite direction to the source of the light!

The shape of the cast shadow will also be a reflection of the shape of the object casting the shadow; In this case it is a straight sided cube so the shadow will reflect those straight lines.

Practice this by shading the cube you drew in Exercise 3 and work out for yourself why the different sides of the cube are dark or light and why the shadow looks like it does.

If you walk around and look for the shadows cast by objects in your home, in the garden or the street, you will see this to be true. Often the object is illuminated by more than one light source, such as two windows. This will result in two shadows, one for each light source. It's important to understand this as it helps you to analyze what you are seeing.

The sphere

In classic drawing classes the student is taught that there are two types of light: Direct light including highlights, and reflected light.

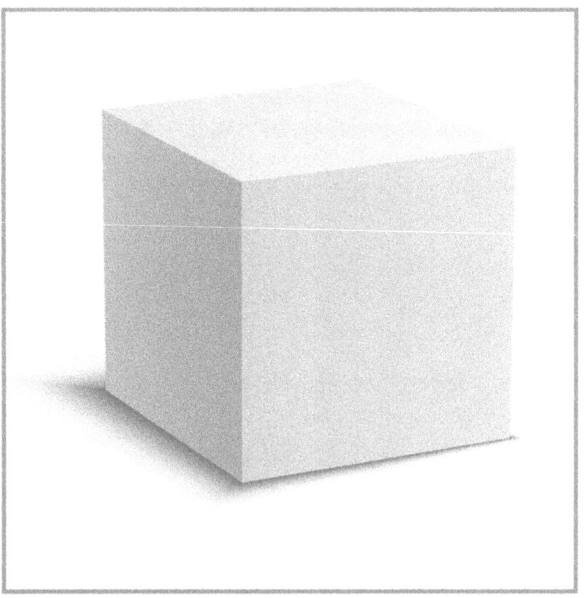

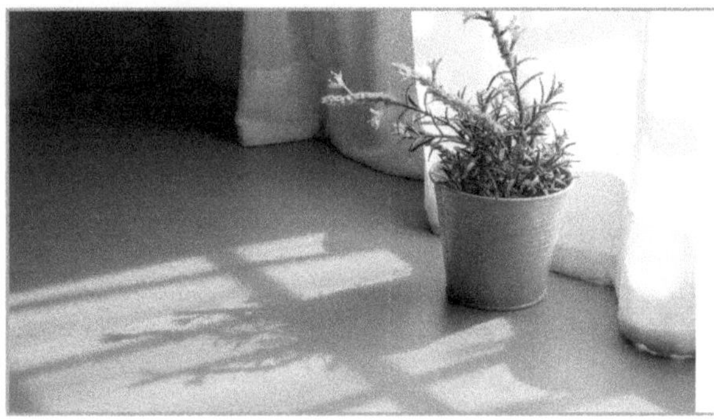

In the photo above you can observe that the light source is coming from the right through the window and the shadows are on the opposite side of the wall and plant.

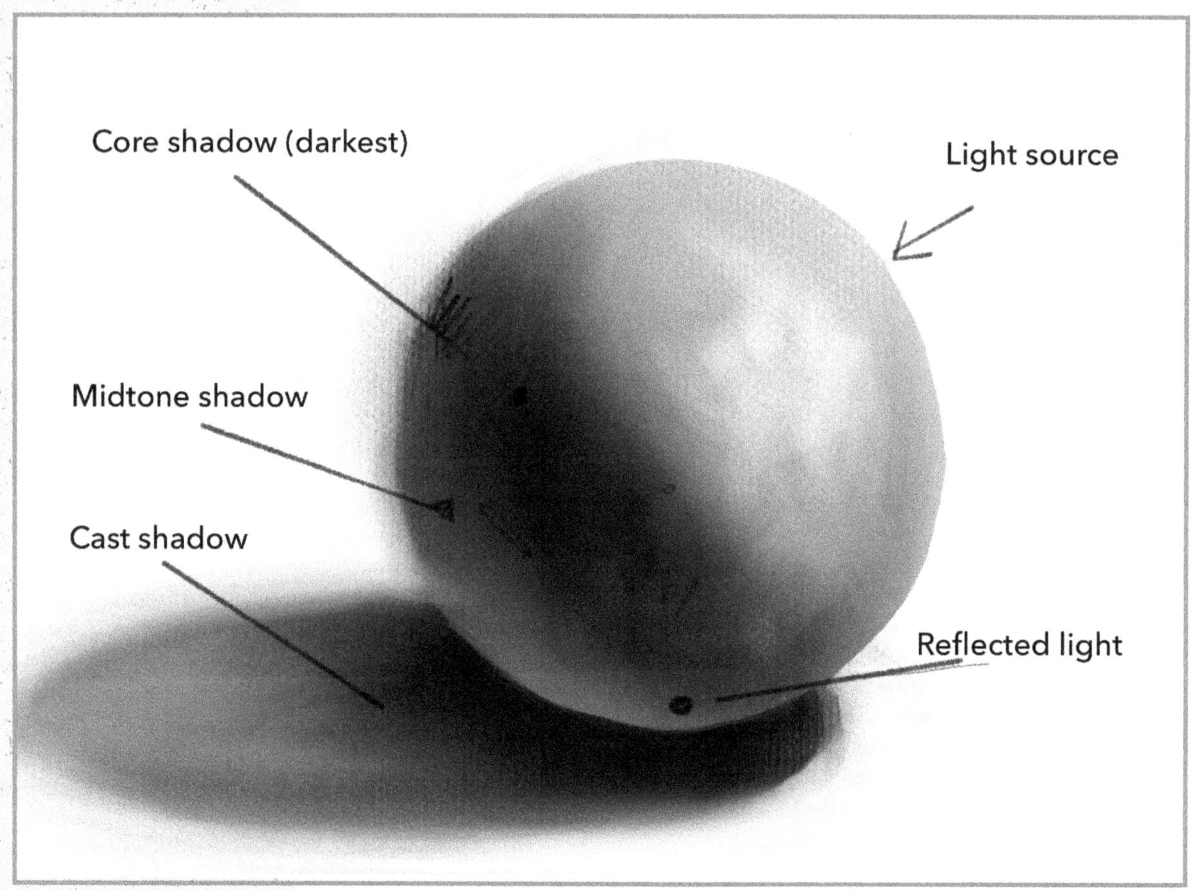

This is important whenever you are drawing spherical objects.

This illustration demonstrates reflected light compared to direct light and highlights.

Reflected light is the light that bounces back off the ground and hits the shaded area underneath the object, hence the term reflected light.

If you have a good light source and an orange or apple you can see this for yourself. It might be easier if you take a photo of it and turn the photo black and white.

Grasping the concept of reflected light helps you analyze tonal values of objects around you, especially spheres, cones and cylinders.

Shade in the sphere you drew in the last lesson. Do your best to include reflected light, and also notice the shape of the shadow it casts will be elliptical, reflective of the circular form of the sphere.

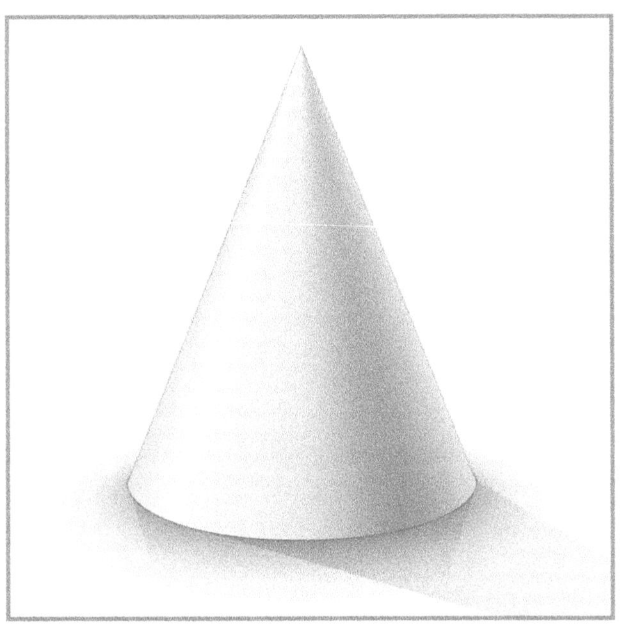

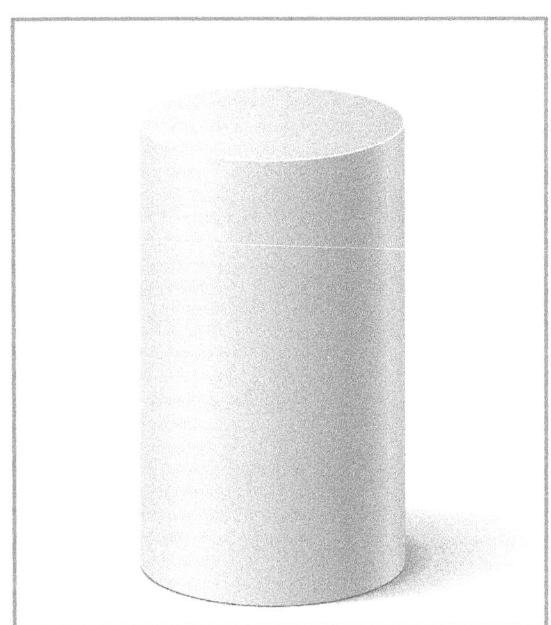

Once you have shaded in the three primary forms, you can finish off the lesson by shading in the remainder of the forms you drew following the examples provided.

Next comes the cone. Again, the shadow will not just be all black one side and white the other, there will be some reflected light within the shadow as shown in the illustration, so make sure you take that into account, along with the shape of the shadow it casts.

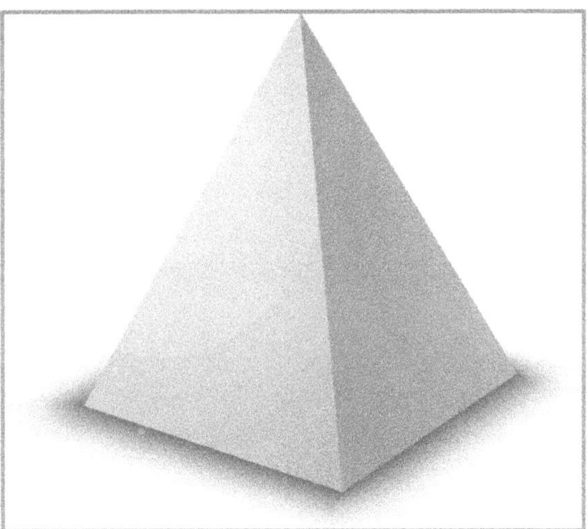

The cylinder is similar, Draw this first using the same procedure you used drawing the shape. Then add the shading.

You can see from the illustration if the four-sided pyramid that the light is coming from the back so both sides are in shadow one more than the other.

FINAL EXERCISE

This chapter has introduced you to the value of breaking down what you see into simple forms. For your final exercise we want you to take out your sketchbook and start breaking down things you see into simple lines, shapes and forms, and then adding shading based on the light source. Do not worry too much about getting proportions of one thing to another correct - that comes next.

Once you add in the ability to correctly estimate proportions in the next two chapters you will be set to set out on your journey to being able to draw anything, including human forms. In the next three chapters you are going to learn to objectively analyze what you see and break it down into basic lines and shapes.

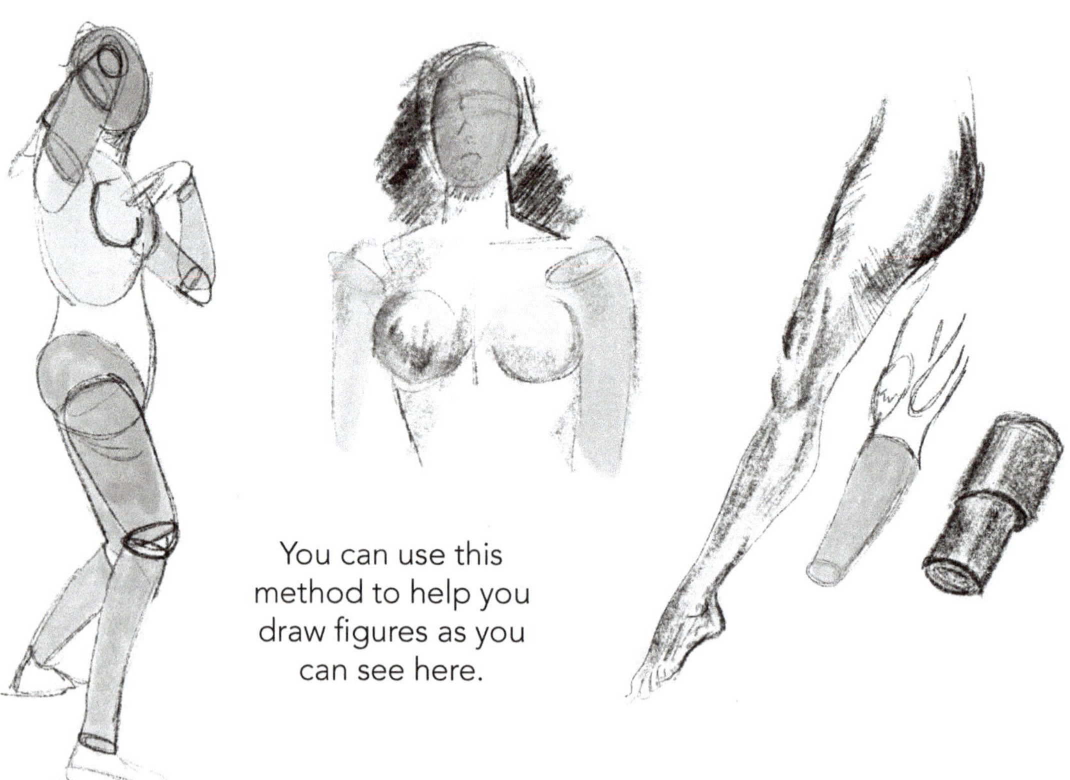

You can use this method to help you draw figures as you can see here.

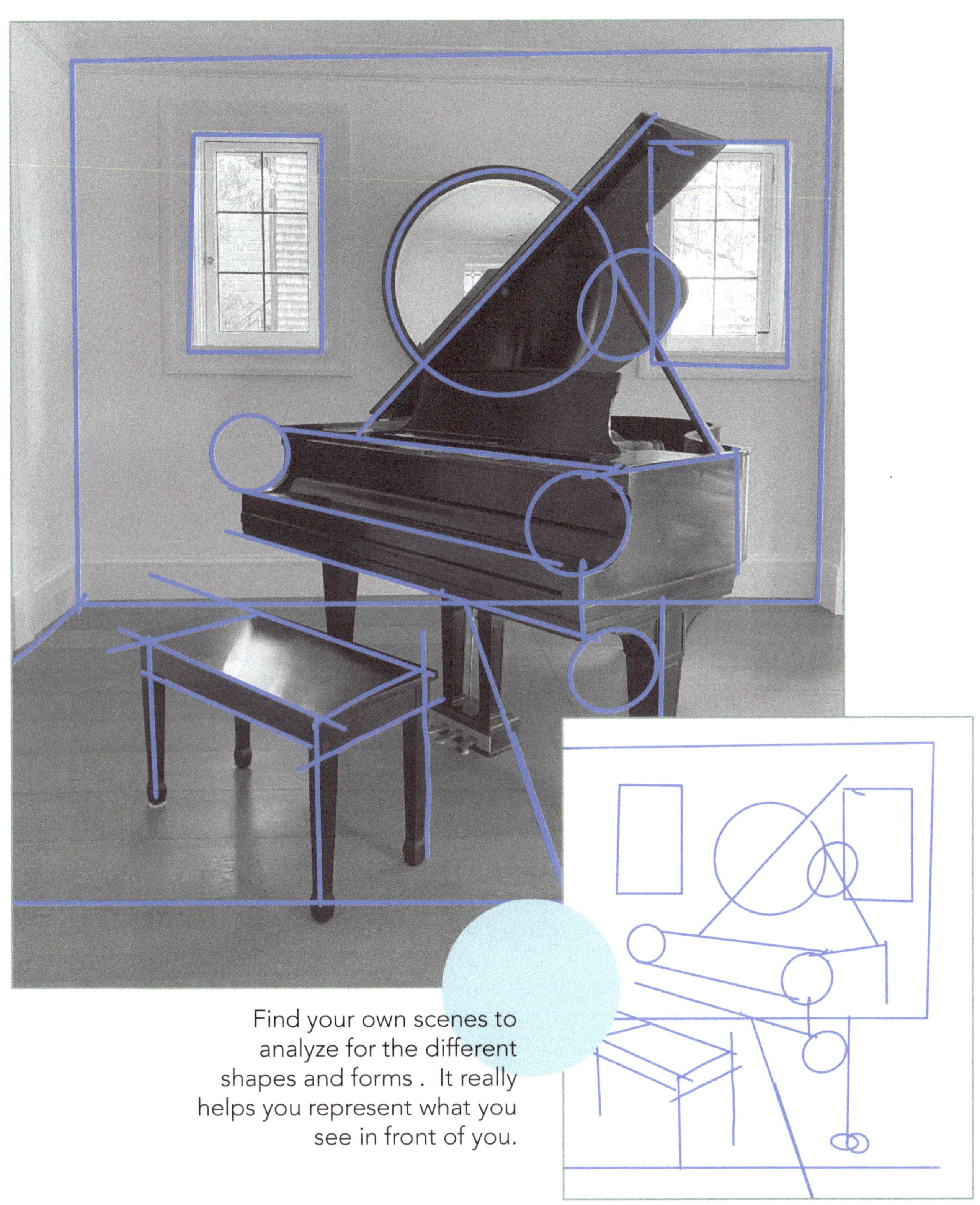

Find your own scenes to analyze for the different shapes and forms . It really helps you represent what you see in front of you.

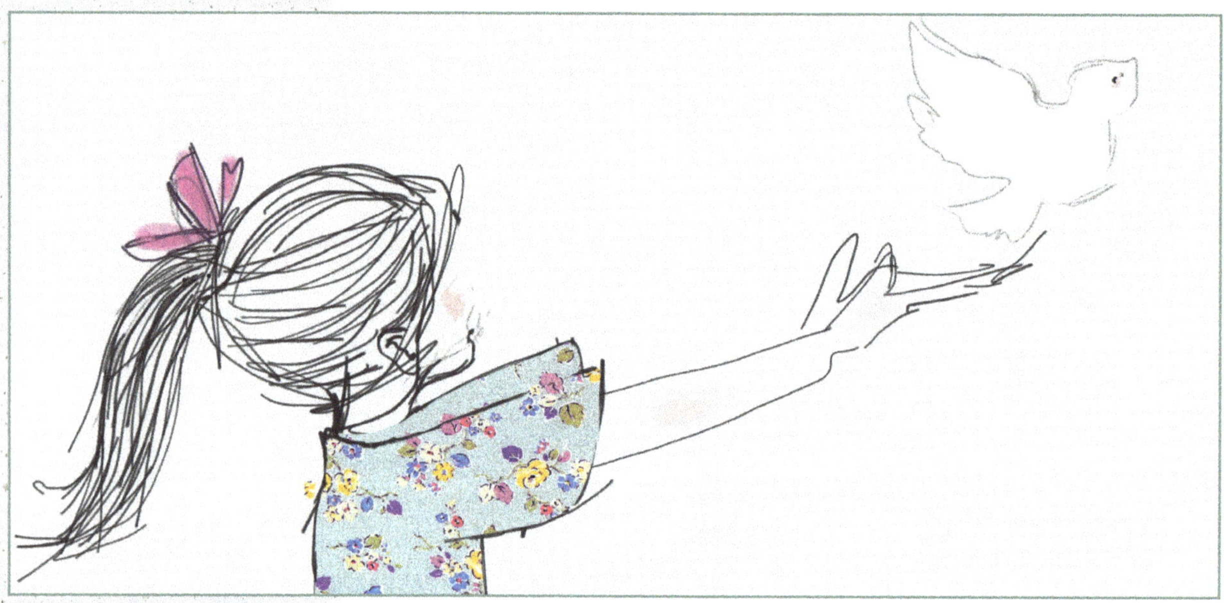

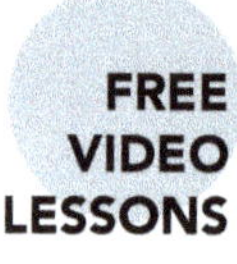

FREE VIDEO LESSONS

Traditional Drawing Video Demonstrations

FREE VIDEO LESSONS

Digital Drawing Video Demonstrations

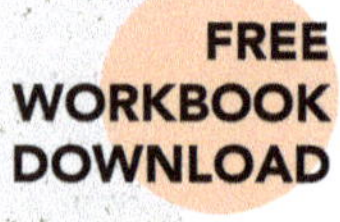

FREE WORKBOOK DOWNLOAD

"Very few people have the ability to identify proportions of a rectangle by simple observation. Usually, analysis and measurement are required.
To calculate the proportion of a work of art or any image, divide the larger number by the smaller number, and it will give you the proportions of the rectangle."

Michael Jacobs
The Art of Composition

Chapter 7: Proportions

The Chapter 4 exercises taught you to use the grid method to get things in the correct proportion, and you did a pretty good job of getting it right! Now it's time to hone your skills so you correctly estimate where things go without the need of a grid.

"Let proportion be found not only in numbers and measures, but also in sounds, weights, times, and positions, and what ever force there is."
Leonardo da Vinci

EXERCISE 1
Estimating proportions

Look at the oblong shape of Katy's lovely drawing on the opposite page. In this exercise you are going to work out how to estimate the proportion of the rectangular frame correctly using only your pencil to do so.

1. Take your pencil and hold it up against the oblong box. With the end of the pencil touching the top left corner and lined up against the left side of the frame, place your thumb or finger on the bottom left corner as in the illustration to the right.

2. Now, without removing your thumb from the pencil, turn the pencil horizontally and see how many times it will fit into the length from left to right.

3. It fits twice, correct? OK, that means the width is twice the height. When we express this as a proportion it will be 1:2

When you draw the oblong on your paper, whatever height you make the oblong, the width will be double. Draw the straight lines following Chapter 1, Exercise 3, How to draw a straight line.

Voilá! Its proportions will be exactly the same as Katy's drawing!

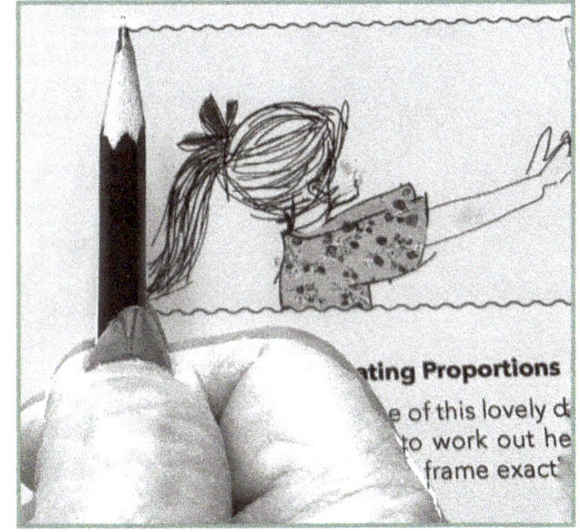

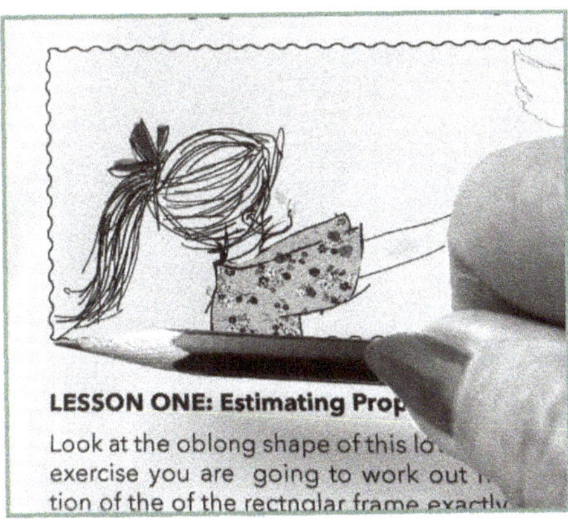

EXERCISE 2
Estimating proportions

Applying the steps you learned in the first exercise we will take this a step further and draw a mug.

How do you draw this mug so it is in perfect proportion? Follow the steps in this lesson and you will be able to!

The first challenge is to estimate the proportion of the oval at the top of the mug, width to height.

From there we will be able to estimate the proportion of the width of the mug to its height and so forth.

Let's get started.

Print off a copy of this photo of a mug from the workbook you can access at the start of this chapter. If you are using an iPad you can download the image to your iPad from our website using the link provided in Section 7 of the workbook.

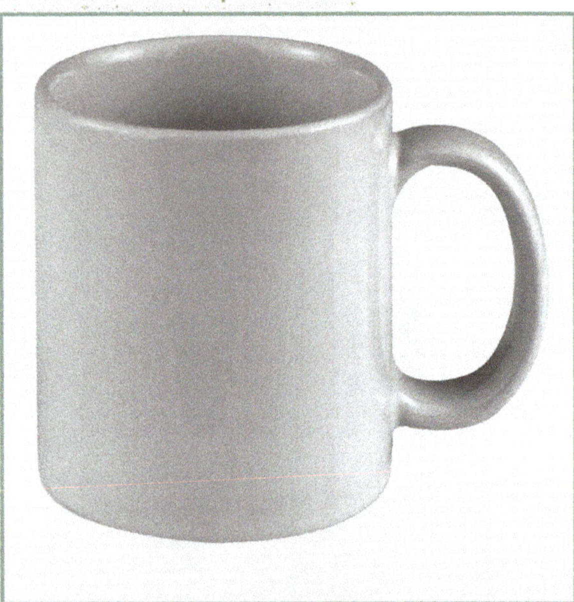

1. Using your pencil as you did in the earlier exercise, measure the height of the oval, then turn your pencil over and, keeping your thumb or finger on the pencil, see how many times you can fit the height into the width. It will fit about 4 times.

2. *NOTE: We are only looking for approximate proportions. To be exact you would have to use a ruler, but we are training you to use your pencil to estimate proportions of the objects you see around you as you will learn in the next chapter.*

3. Now you know the approximate proportion of the height of the oval compared to its width, you're ready to transfer this information to your drawing paper.

4. Firstly, draw a horizontal line about 3/4 up the paper from one side to the other, and

then a vertical line about halfway across the page. Draw these lines very faintly as you will be erasing them later in this exercise. (Figure 1)

5. Mark the left edge of the mug on the horizontal line, and the right edge the same distance from the middle line. This gives you the width of your cup. HINT: leave enough room on the right for the handle of the mug.

6. From your pencil measurement, you know the height of the oval is approximately one quarter of the width, so mark this on the vertical line - half above the center and half below as shown in figure 1.

7. Lightly sketch in the oval by connecting the dots! Use the lesson on drawing a circle from Chapter One and lightly sketch the ellipse so it passes through each of the marks you made as shown in Figure 2.

8. Next, you need to estimate the height of the mug compared to its width, once again using the photo.

9. Use your pencil to mark the full width of the oval and then turn the pencil over and see how many times you can fit that into the left side of the mug on the photo. You will see the height of the mug is about the same as its width - maybe a tiny bit longer.

You can now transfer this information to your drawing.

1. First of all sketch in the sides of the mug on your drawing using straight lines that go from the edge of the oval downwards.

2. Estimate the height of the mug by using your pencil to measure the full width of the oval in your drawing, and then rotate

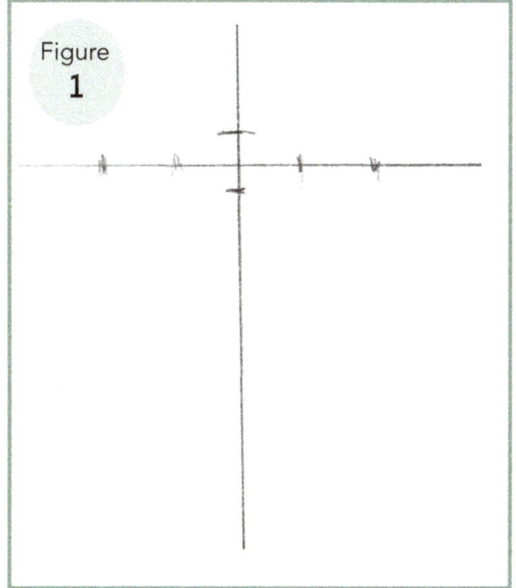

Figure 1

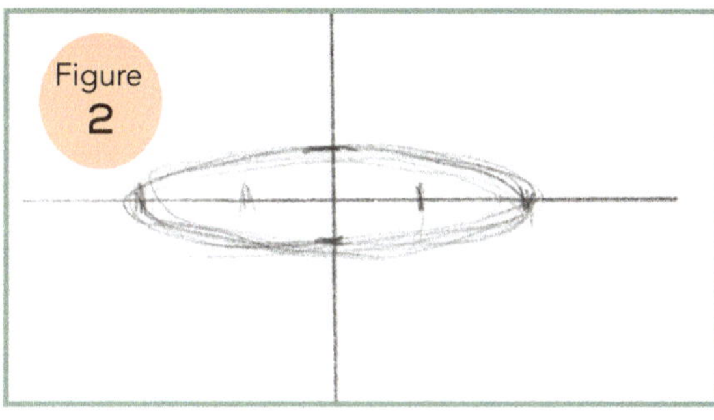

Figure 2

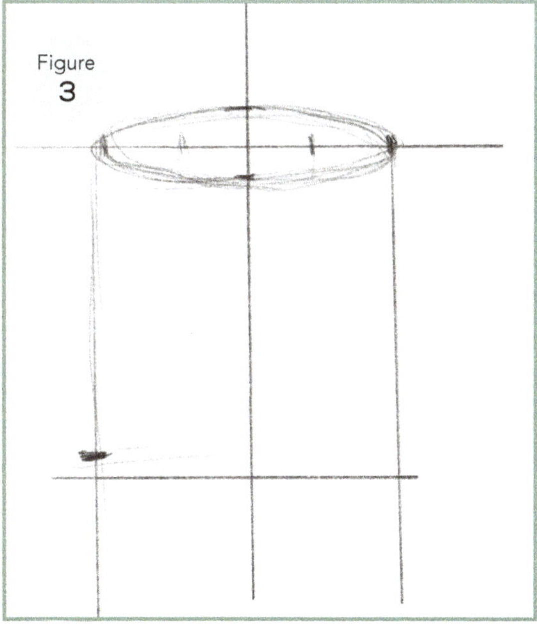

Figure 3

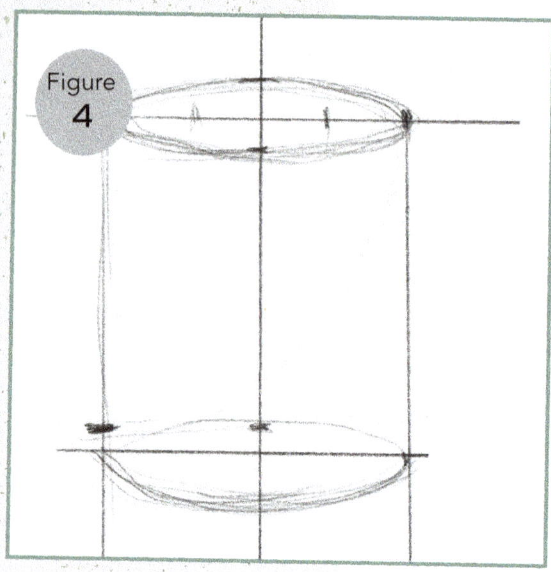

Figure 4

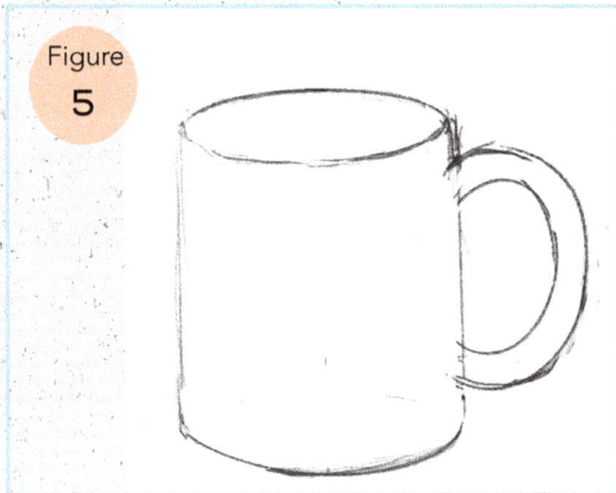

Figure 5

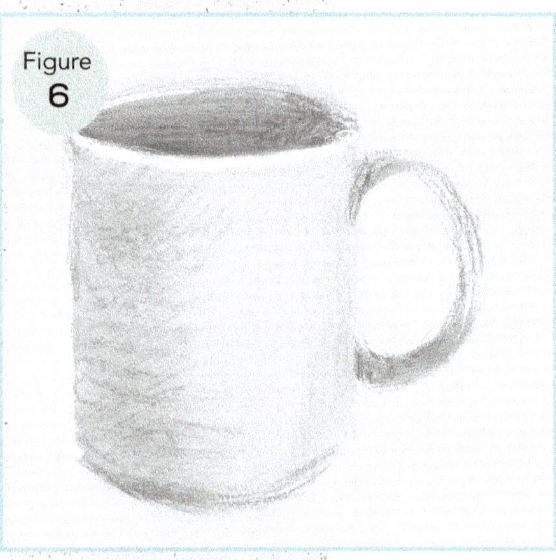

Figure 6

the pencil and use that measurement to note the bottom edge of the cup on the left. Remember it will be just a little longer than the width. Make a mark on the vertical line on the left of the drawing.

3. Now, draw a horizontal line that intersects the right edge of the cup as shown in Figure 3.

4. This now allows you to duplicate the oval you drew at the top of the cup, using the exact same proportions as shown in Figure 4.

5. Erase the guidelines and you will have the simple outlines for the mug, minus the handle.

Sketch in the outlines of the handle using the same method of estimating its proportions.

6. Go back to your photo and use the shorter measurement of the height of the oval to estimate the approximate position of the handle, top and bottom, and the width of the handle and so forth.

7. Transfer this information to your drawing, making marks to indicate location of the handle, top and bottom (Hint - it is about the same as the height of the oval!). Then repeat this to figure out the shape of the handle and so forth. HINT: if your sketch doesn't look right, go back and repeat your estimation of proportions and redo it. Keep your pencil lines very light so you can easily erase until you are happy with it.

Once you have your light sketch of outlines correct, you can finish up your drawing to make it look more three dimensional, using the shading skills learned in Chapter 3 and Chapter 6 where you shaded in the cylinder. Refer back to the photo to finish up your drawing and make sure to erase any unneeded guidelines.

Whew!!! That was a real workout!!!

FINAL EXERCISE

For your final exercise, you will draw a still life, using your pencil as a way to figure out how large one object is compared to another object in the photo.

We suggest you start with the large white jug and draw a horizontal line to mark off the top and a vertical line to mark the middle and then use your pencil to estimate proportions.

Alternately, if you prefer, you can start with the pear on the far right. It doesn't really matter. Just select something and start.

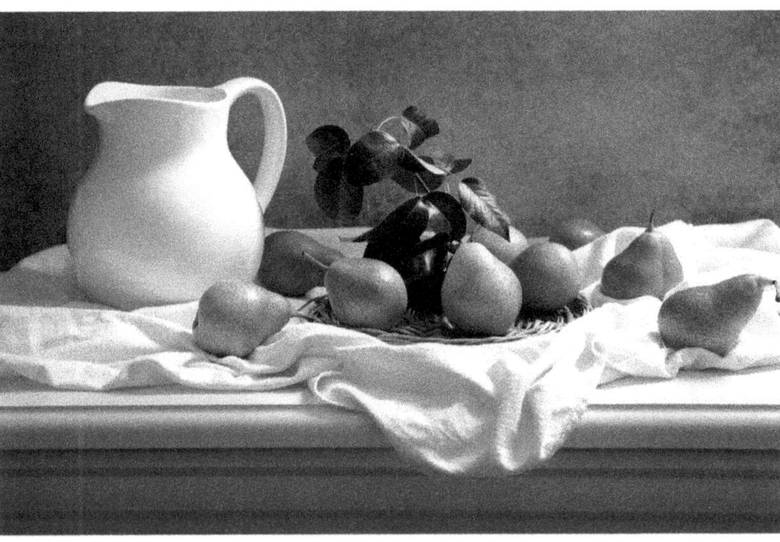

Print this photo from Section 7 of the workbook or, if you are using an iPad, use the link provided to access and download it from our website.

Once you have the first object sketched in, the other objects can be compared to it, again using your pencil to work out where they go and their proportions.

Use light sketching lines so you an easily erase and redo it, and when you are happy use your honed-in shading skills to finish it up.

Voilá! You will have your first solo drawing done without the need of a grid or tracing. You are well on your way. The next chapter will round out this skill so you are ready to draw anything and everything!

FREE VIDEO LESSONS

Traditional Drawing Video Demonstrations

FREE VIDEO LESSONS

Digital Drawing Video Demonstrations

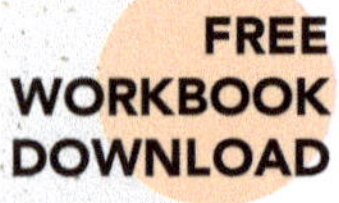

FREE WORKBOOK DOWNLOAD

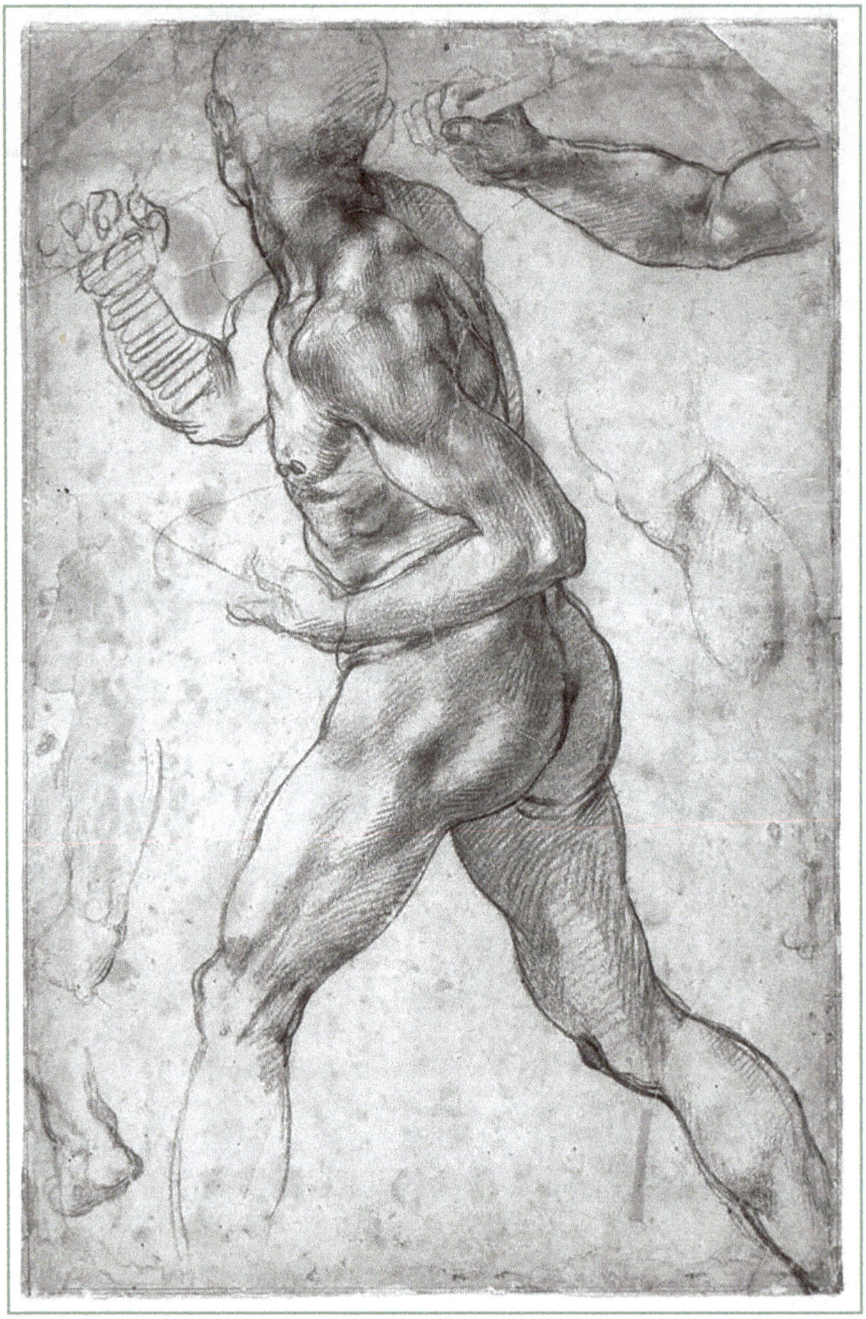

Michelangelo Buonarroti "Striding Male Nude, and Anatomical Details, 1504 or 1506

Chapter 8: Drawing Without a Net

Up until now, we have concentrated on providing you with the skills to represent a 3D object on a 2D page, and how to correctly estimate where things go with and without a tracing or grid. In the last chapter, we showed you that your pencil is far more important than simply a mark-making tool. However, ultimately, all of this is leading to the point where you can sit in front of something and draw it as-is, without the safety net of a grid or tracing. It takes practice, but there is a definite joy in being able to draw things as you see them in real life.

Let's review what you have learned so far!

In the previous chapters we focused on the key fundamentals of learning how to draw.

- In the first chapter you found out all pencils are not the same. You learned how to hold your pencil, how to draw straight and curvy lines, all of which are needed for the subsequent chapters.

- In the second chapter you learned the skill of using different marks and textures to create shading whilst interpreting the character of different objects you are drawing.

- In the third chapter you learned about light and shadow and why it is so important to make something look three-dimensional.

- The fourth chapter introduced you to gridding and the idea of looking and seeing the relationship of objects around you, and how they intersect with one line and shape with another.

- In the fifth chapter you learned to use charcoal, freeing you up to express yourself through line and contrasting shapes.

- In the last chapter we took a big leap forward, learning to use your pencil to help you estimate proportions by using photographs.

"An artist must have his measuring tools not in the hand, but in the eye."
Michelangelo

Now in the seventh and final chapter, we will revisit the subject of using your pencil to measure what you see. You will learn to estimate relative sizes, angles, and intersections of what you see in front of you. This skill is so valuable that we are dedicating this whole chapter to it.

You will be drawing real objects - ones around you in your home, but also in museums, parks, and so forth. In this chapter, you should get busy with your sketchbook and start drawing everything you see. With this skill under your belt, it is a matter of practice, practice, practice.

So let's get busy!

Your pencil plays two different functions in drawing

We have introduced you to both of these roles. Your pencil is a tool to create marks, but it is also a tool for estimating proportions as you learned in the last lesson.

We will expand your ability to use your pencil in its second role which will enable you to draw anything you see.

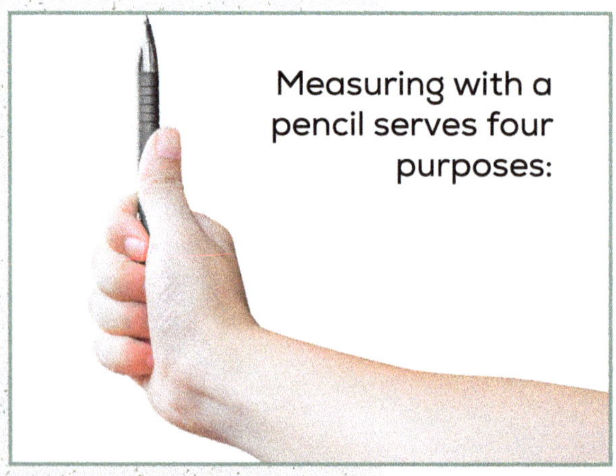

1. Measuring proportions on a model;

2. Checking proportions in a drawing;

3. Measuring angles on a model and checking them in your drawing;

4. Checking the cross-sections and points where one line crosses another, both on a model and in your drawing.

As covered in the previous chapter, measuring proportions is the process of analyzing how many times one part of an object fits into another part.

Measuring angles involves checking the tilts of certain lines.

Checking cross-sections and cross-points entails finding and checking where certain lines intersect other lines. This is similar to what you learned in gridding, except you are using your pencil as your "live" grid.

Over time you develop the ability to measure proportions and angles by eye without the need of measuring tools. This will happen automatically over time, but only if you practice.

When you apply these drawing principles, you can draw objects, judging the proportions and angles by eye, and then double-check by measuring with a pencil.

Setting up your model for drawing

The best way to start is to use yourself as a model. But for this you will need a large wall mirror which you can set up so you can see yourself reflected in it.   Either that, or get a friend to sit still for you.

Or you can employ the time tested method of using statues to perfect this skill. Look for a statue in your nearest park or art museum. Most museums will have such statues cast in bronze or plaster, or even original works. We selected a statue by Rodin displayed in Stanford University's Cantor Museum. Most museums welcome students and will even provide a stool for you if you ask. If not, take a little portable stool

Sit in front of a wall mirror and hold up your pencil to compare the size of one part of your body to another.

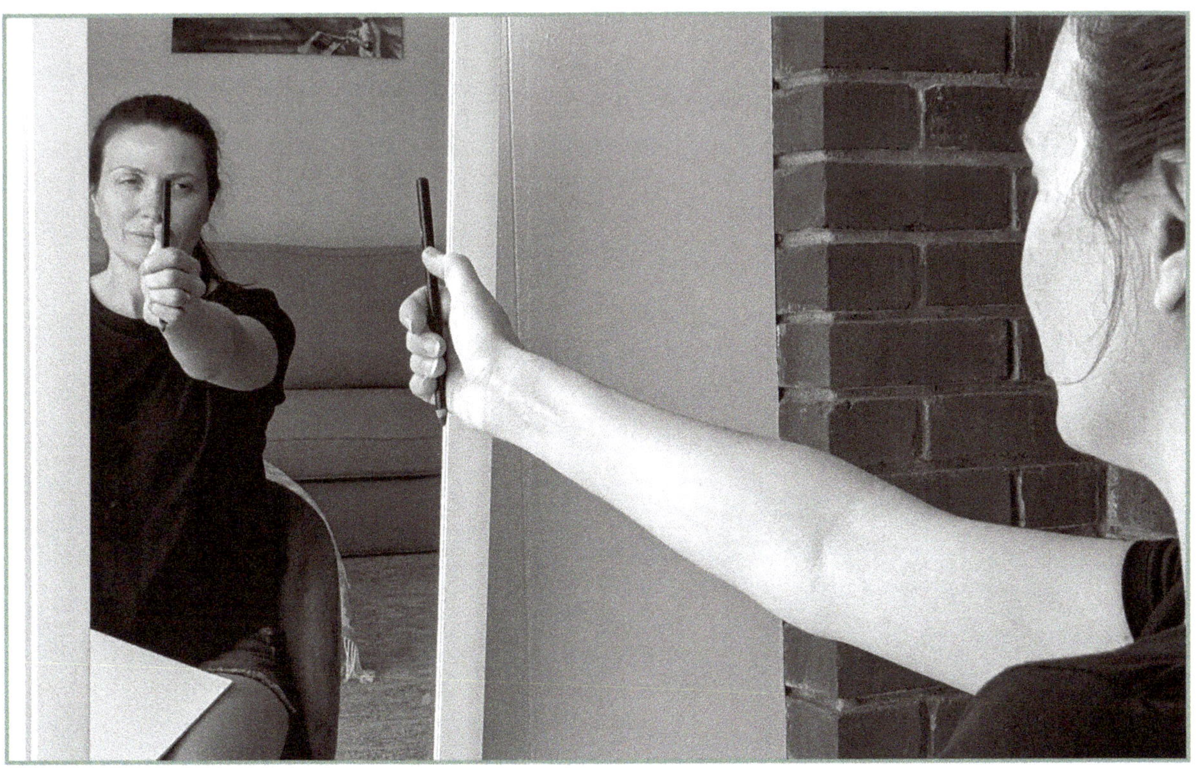

with you and set it up, letting them know what you are doing.

Even if you do start the exercise using yourself or your friend, going to a museum or park to draw the statues is great practice for the future.

Don't be despondent if your initial drawings are not the greatest. But keep them so you can track your progress.

DRAWING WITHOUT A NET

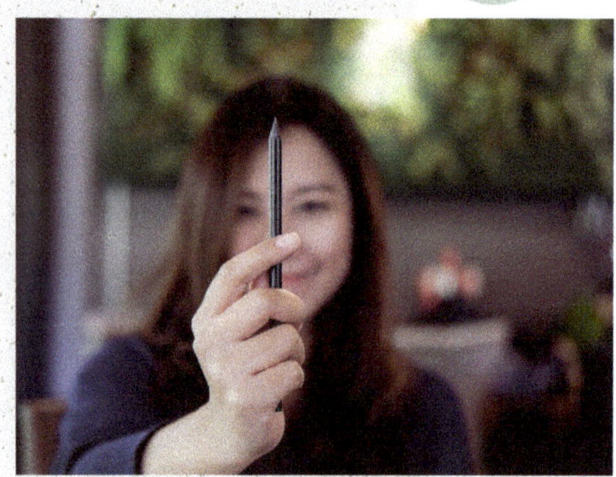

In this exercise you will either be drawing yourself in the mirror, a live model or a statue. But, either way you are going to be drawing without the help of photos, grids or tracing. Your only prop is your pencil!

Begin by using your pencil to note down important measurements. Extend your arm fully while holding your pencil with the "drumstick' grip as shown in this photo. The pencil can be positioned vertically, horizontally or tilted left or right,but not forward or backward.

Close one eye and, squinting through the other one, align the pencil with the model or object. Move your thumb along the pencil so that your measurement fits between the edge of the pencil and the tip of your thumb.

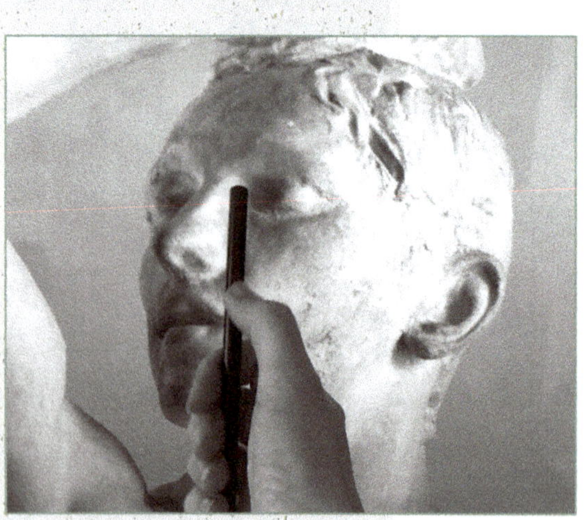

Now, keeping your thumb in place, align the pencil with another, larger portion of the model or object. See how many times the first size fits into the new one, just as you did in the previous chapter with the photo of the mug.

In this way, you can check different proportion: how many times the head of the model fits into the body, and so on.

When you do this you will start noticing spatial relationships you did not see before. For example, in most faces the eyes come halfway down the shape of the head. If you didn't use your pencil you would likely draw the eyes much higher up on the head and your drawing would not look anatomically correct.

Checking proportions in a drawing

When you know what a given proportion is, you can double-check it in your drawing.

Take your pencil and align it with the given dimension in the drawing.

Using your index finger, mark this dimension on the pencil.

Keeping your finger still, re-align the pencil with the larger dimension you checked on the model.

Check how many times the smaller dimension in your drawing fits into the larger one.

Needless to say, the ratio between these two dimensions has to be the same in your drawing and on the model. If not, fix the drawing.

Measure angles on a model and check them in your drawing

Here, we are interested in angles and tilts rather than dimensions and proportions.

Position your drawing board vertically at arm's length, so you can see the model and the drawing at the same time.

Fully extend your arm while holding your pencil with a paintbrush grip.

With one eye closed, align the pencil with the angle you want to measure on the model or object. Do not tilt the pencil forward or backward, it has to be perpendicular to your line of sight. Without changing the tilt of the pencil, move your straight arm towards the drawing and check whether the tilt aligns with the given angle in your art-

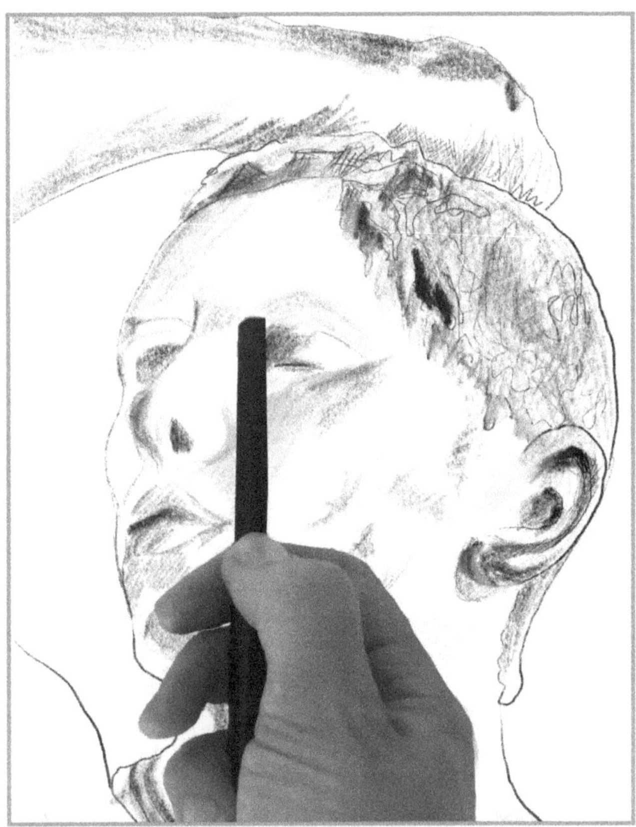

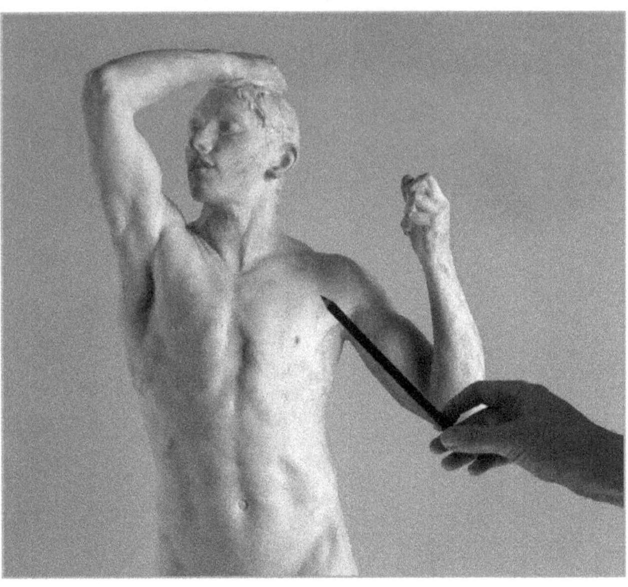

Use your pencil to estimate angles of different objects such as this arm.

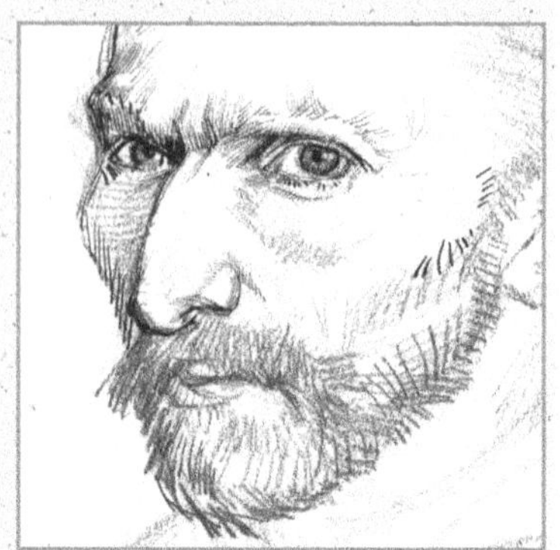

Drawing by Vincent Van Gogh

"If you hear a voice within you say 'you cannot paint then by all means paint, and that voice will be silenced,"
Vincent Van Gogh

work. If not, fix the angle in your drawing.

Checking cross-sections and points where one line crosses or intersects with another, both on a model and in your drawing

This measurement is similar to the previous exercise. However, instead of checking only angles, this time you need to analyze points of intersection.

Use the same vertical position as a drawing board as in the previous process.

Extend your arm as you did to measure angles on the model.

Align the pencil with the object in question on the model and check where the pencil intersects with other parts of the model.

A good example of this method is, when drawing a still-life, you can extend with a pencil the line of one part of the model and check where it intersects with another part - the shoulder with the knee for example.

Finally, use your pencil to verify proportions, angles and intersections in your drawing, fixing them if required.

FINAL DRAWING CHALLENGE

Your final drawing challenge is to execute five live drawings of different scenes around you, indoors or outdoors Whether it's a still life, landscape or a sketch of your favorite pet, the only stipulation is to draw with only your pencil to support you,

Use all the skills you have learned, and if you are dissatified with a drawing, don't give up. Go back over the chapters of the book and see which skill you need to improve.

Don't fall into the trap of being overly critical of your drawings. This is a journey, not a destination. Take Vincent's advice from the quote in the margin and when you feel like giving up, just keep drawing and that inner critic will be silenced.

Throughout your journey keep applying the mantra of our book: No pressure, no judgment and you will experience the pure joy of drawing!

A word about digital drawing

Both Katy and I are digital artists as well as using traditional tools to draw and paint. We met at one of my classes that showed people how to use art apps on their iPad, the main one being Procreate, and we instantly became friends.

I was introduced to drawing and painting on my iPad when we first moved to the Bay Area of California, and I immediately fell in love with the process and began teaching in many different art institutions and groups. My own website has an entire section dedicated to my digital paintings and drawings and you can view it at www.carolinemustard.com.

We encourage all digital artists to study this book use their iPad or phone as their drawing pad and sketchbook. Use the sketching tools with an Apple pencil and you will see how you can simulate the drawing experience.

We also have a six-part instructional video series called Procreate® Basics that walks you through the different drawing and painting tools and how to use them.

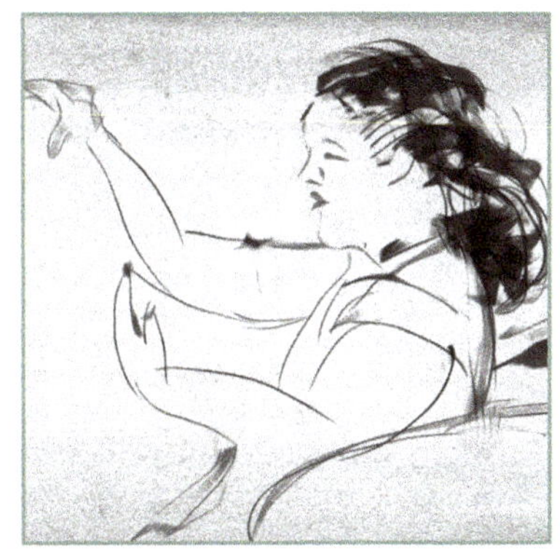

Deb drawing on her iPad. I drew this on my iPad using the Sketch Club® painting app.

"Who would have thought that the telephone would bring back drawing?"
David Hockney

You can purchase the series by visiting our website: **www.thejoyofdrawing.org** where you will find the series in the Store's Video Library.

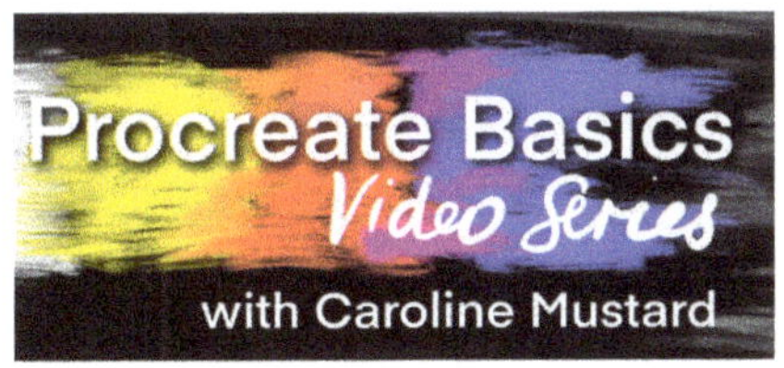

*Traditional Drawing Video
Demonstrations*

*Digital Drawing Video
Demonstrations*

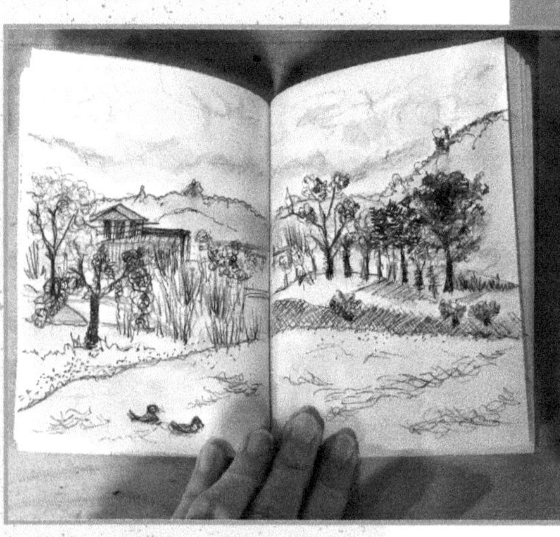

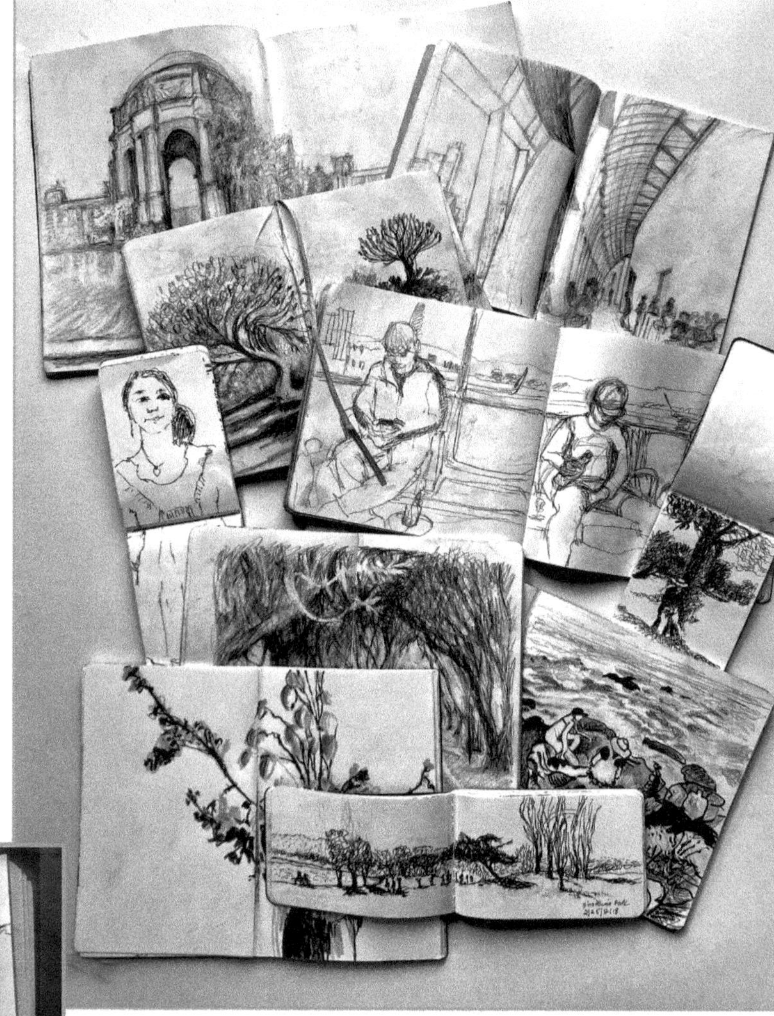

Above: These sketchbooks only represent a few in my collection, but it goes to show you that the books become a visual journal of your journey through life.

On the left, Katy's sketch is one of many we did together on our Art Hiking class.

Chapter 9: Sketching

From the outset of these lessons we recommended you purchase a sketchbook. If you didn't get one yet, then this is the time to do it. Because this class is all about the importance of having a sketchbook close to you at all times so you can follow our best advice on improving your drawing skills.

Three Golden Rules

- Sketch Everything,

- Sketch Everywhere,

- Sketch Everyday!

In the Introduction to this book we repeated wise advice we both received from our respective art instructors who made us use a sketchbook and sketch everyday.

There is a side benefit to this: Your sketch books become a living record of your life.

I have amassed many sketchbooks, and sometimes I look through them. Not only do I see my own skills improving, I also revisit people, places and moments in time.

I have lots of different things in my sketchbooks. Sometimes the page is upside down. Sometimes I scribble a note about needing to buy milk while I am out, or a telephone number. And on the same page I will find a sketch and each time it is a memory.

I also use my sketchbook to draw out ideas for paintings and can rapidly sketch several thumbnail drawings with different concepts and compositions.

I also use my phone as a sketchbook when I am traveling using several apps on my iPhone˚: Procreate Pocket˚, and Paper˚ are my favorites. Each has its own unique quality. Another benefit from using your iPhone while on a train ride or sitting at the airport. I call this stealth sketching as no one knows you are drawing - they just think you are checking emails or

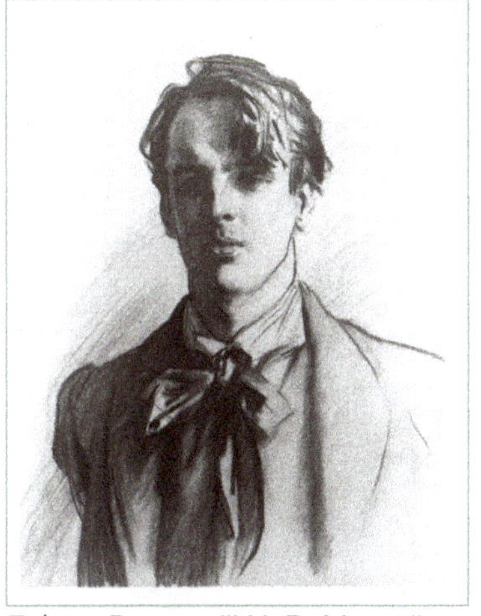

Edgar Degas "W. B. Yeats" (1908)

"You can't do sketches enough. Sketch everything and keep your curiosity fresh."
John Singer Sargent

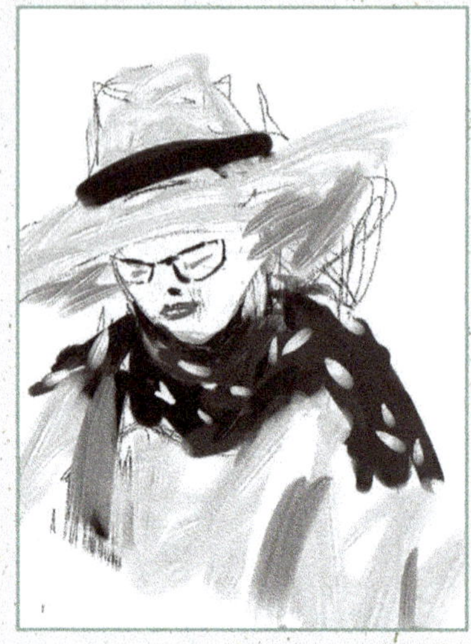

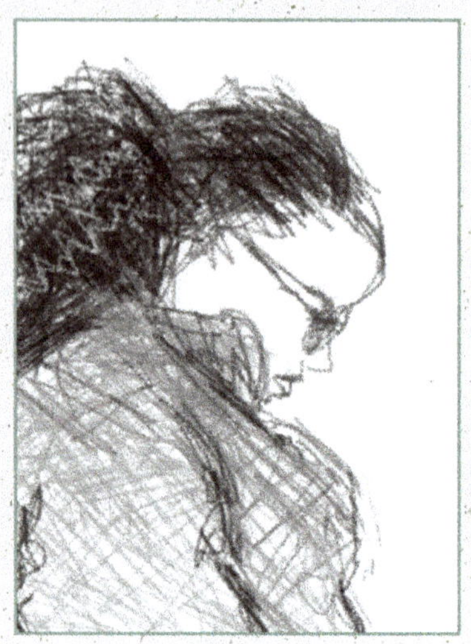

These are both sketches done by Caroline on her iPhone with the Procreate app.

texts or looking at social media. As a result they don't gather around as some tend to do when they see you drawing in a sketchbook. This also means they don't know when the subject of your sketch is them!

Sometimes I show the person I sketched the drawing if I think they might like it. They are always pleased.

The point is that sketching is a process of looking. And by looking you expand your visual vocabulary by leaps and bounds.

I prefer sketch books that are bound like books. I like to keep them intact, not pull out pages as you do with a spiral bound book. I like to keep a record of everything, good and bad.

I also like small sketchbooks that I can drop into my purse or backpack along with a couple of pencils, a sharpener and an eraser. Then I'm all set. If you have to lug around large books and tons of pencils then you are too weighted down, and it makes it too important. No, make it so easy to carry around with you so you have NO excuses not to draw.

Sometimes it works to set a time of day for yourself to do some daily drawing or sketching. For me, I just force myself to draw even if I don't want to or I am distracted by other things to do. But, the moment I settle down and start drawing, then the joy of it sets in and you cannot drag me away.

It also doesn't much matter what you draw, just draw. Find things around you. Like your hand! Do not be surprised how hard it is to draw your hand, but if you use the techniques from the last chapter you will get better and better at it.

Drawing is not just a journey, it is also a challenge. If it was easy, then we wouldn't do it. I like to set myself things to draw that are difficult. It starts out terrible, but it gets better, and the more I look, the more I see and understand and then can do.

However you do it, the way to keep going on your drawing journey is to get yourself a sketchbook and draw, draw, draw.

Draw things you are interested in, things you love, things that fascinate you.

Draw small things to start with, and notice relationships.

The important point is, never give up. Feeling like your sketch or drawing is not good enough is just part of the journey. If it was easy, it wouldn't be worth the effort. Wanting to put your pencil down and give up is the point where the rubber meets the road on this journey. It is the point where you MUST keep going. And if you keep going you will learn something and honestly, you will be glad you did.

The joy of drawing is a reflection of the joy of living, seeing and creating. It is an intensively personal journey, and your sketchbooks will be a living record of its ups and downs; its losses, victories and of course its joys.

We want to thank you for traveling on this journey thus far. We hope you will join us again for further books as we release them in order to further your skills.

So it's not goodbye, it's see you again soon!

"My idea of Heaven is to wake up, have a good breakfast, and spend the rest of the day drawing."
Peter Falk

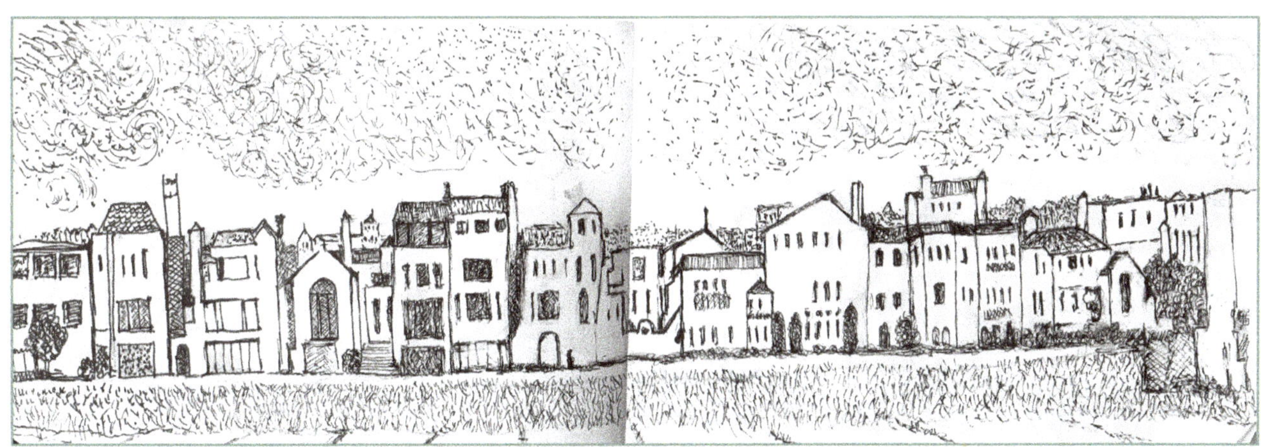

Caroline's outdoor sketch of the homes along the Marina in San Francisco.

The JOY of DRAWING

Where art meets community

We hope you have enjoyed this book as much as we enjoyed creating it. Since its initial publication in 2020, we have been tremendously encouraged by the response from those who have joined us on our creative journey.

To meet the increasing demand for our drawing classes and workshops we established The Joy of Drawing, Inc. — a non profit organization with a mission to empower folks everywhere to learn to draw and experience the joy that it brings.

Visit our website and explore our live streamed and in person workshops and classes as well as our recorded lesson series and workshops.

Workshops & Classes

- Calendar of Live streamed themed workshops

- Monthly online Figure Drawing for Beginners

- Library of recorded workshops and video lessons

- In-person workshops and classes

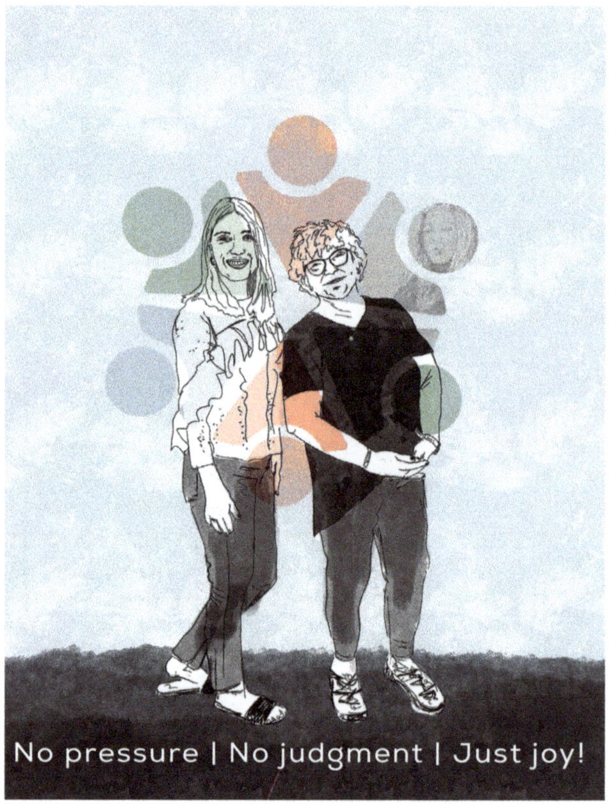

Our Mission

We believe that drawing is the catalyst to discover and nurture your creativity and we have designed our books, live-streamed and in-person workshops and classes to inspire your creative practice and build your confidence at each step.
We strive to bring these experiences to people everywhere - whether you are a complete novice or an experienced hand - you are welcome here.

Visit us at
www.thejoyofdrawing.org

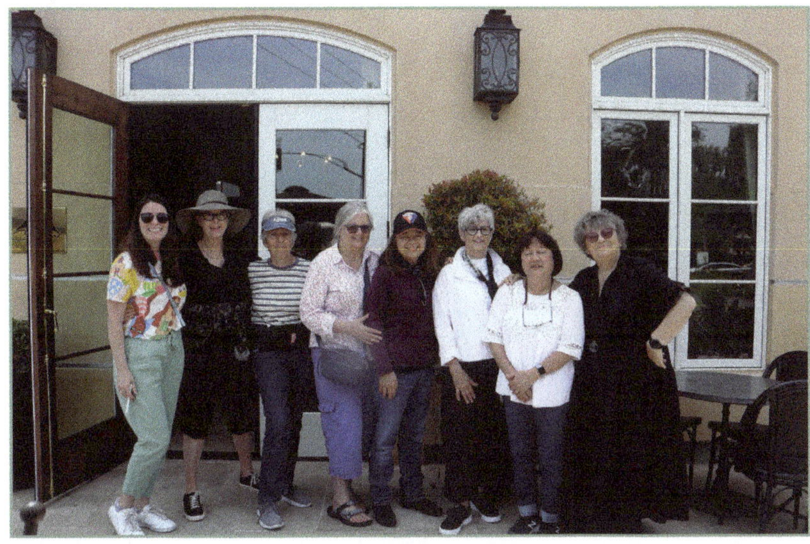

The Joy of Drawing Club

The Joy of Drawing Club was founded in 2018 by Caroline Mustard and Katy Lea, co-authors of The Joy of Drawing book and video series, as a place people could meet up both in person and online with like minded folks. It is for all levels of students from beginners to the more experienced.

Our non-profit initiative

Over the past several years The Joy of Drawing has established a proven system and curriculum that has brought the therapeutic benefits of drawing into the lives of many individuals in California's Bay area and beyond.

We are now embarked on a mission to bring our books, workshops and classes to as many people as we can, especially those who may not have easy access to art supplies or education

Your support will help us pursue our mission of making art more accessible to all.

You can do so at www.thejoyofdrawing.org/donate

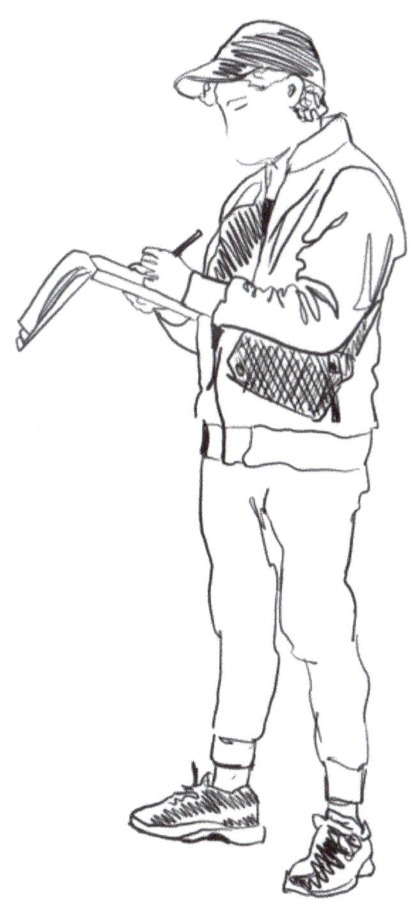

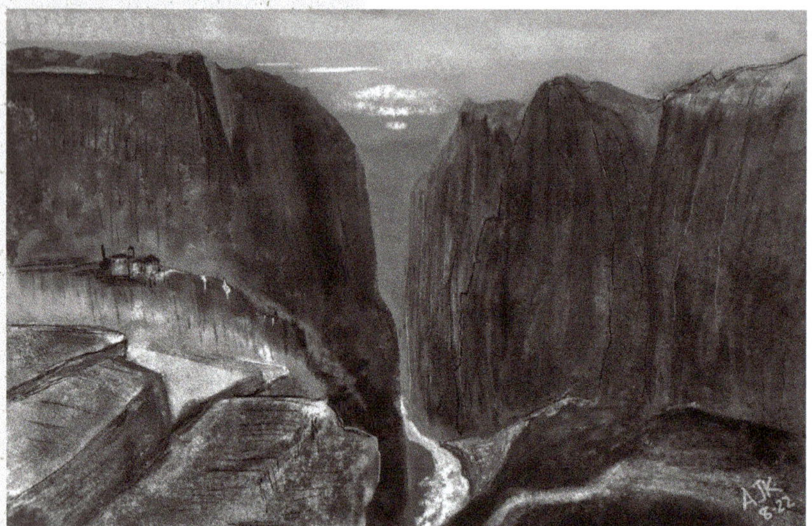

After Edward Lear Drawing

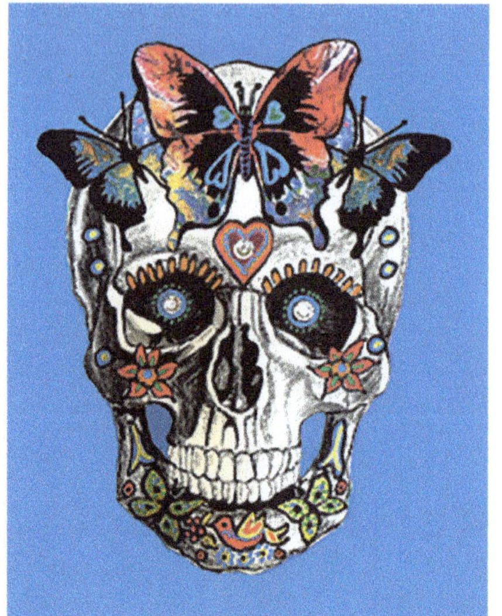

Day of the Dead

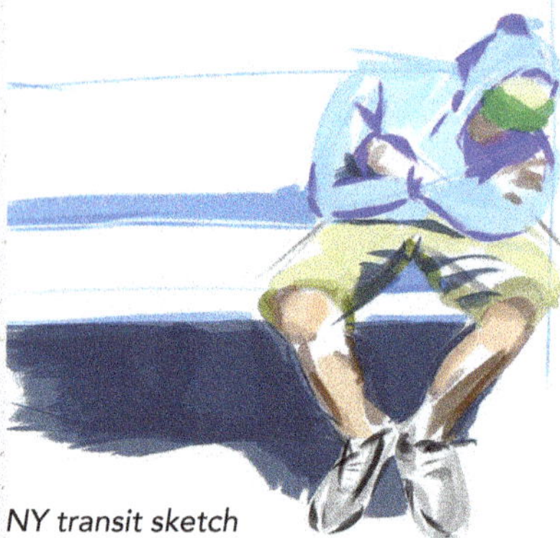

NY transit sketch

A small selection of student work demonstrating different tools and techniques taught throughout this book. From left to righ:
Top: Alan Kushnir; Anne Syer.
Middle: Robyn Setzen; Donna Fleming.

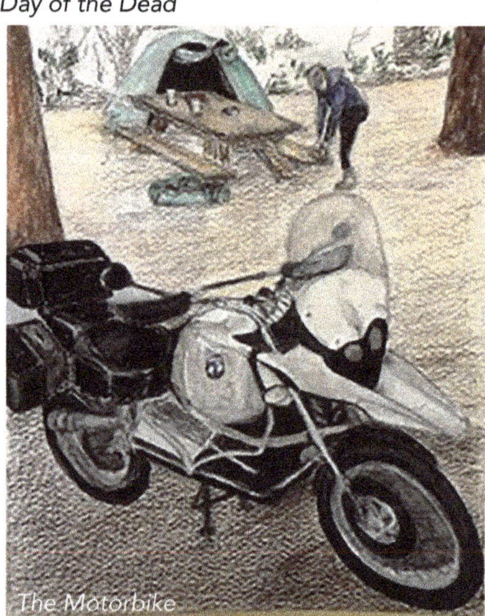

The Motorbike

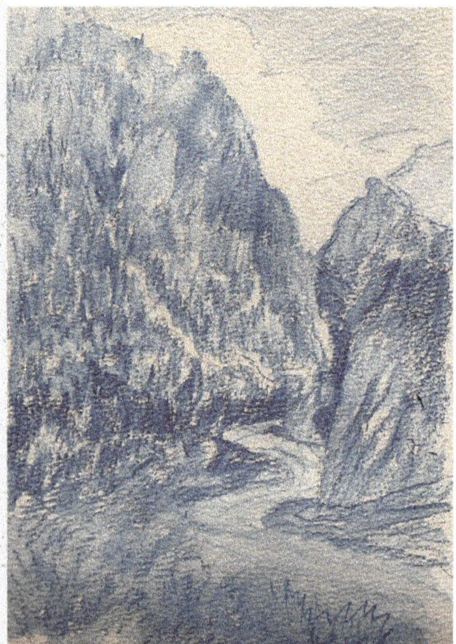

The Road to Mount Whitney

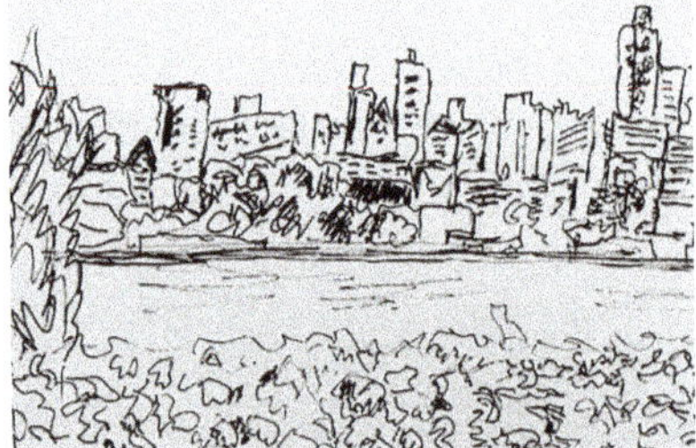

Pein Air sketch of New York Skyline

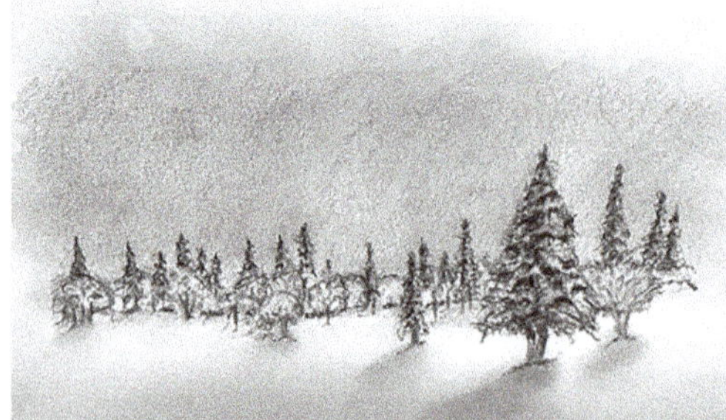

Snowfall

Far left: Sherryl Casella.
Middle: Sylvia Wuensche-Wienands.

Left: Andrew Valentine;
Below: Connie Fotakis.

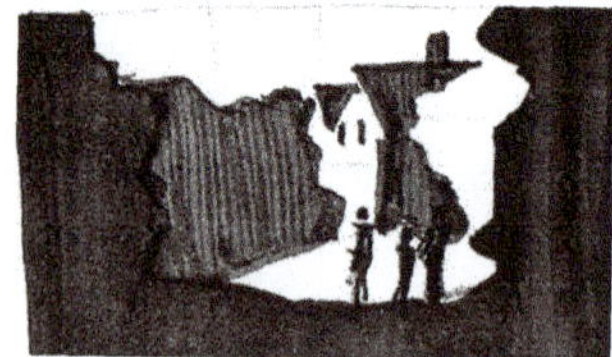

Value study

Book Reviews

The Joy of Drawing book is an amazing resource! I found so many exercises and activities that helps the student learn the ins and outs of drawing with particular focus on different methods for using drawing materials, how to hold the pencil correctly, and how to basically look at the world with fresh eyes. This book is a terrific resource for anyone who wishes to learn to draw!

Donna Dager
Academy of Art University,
San Francisco Faculty

This was just what I needed. With a great deal of fun, I learned how to draw successfully! I amazed myself—I'm someone who worked with their left brain and considered myself to have NO artistic ability. So yes, the book and classes delighted me!

Susan A. Brickey
Retired Executive

Using The Joy of Drawing as a guide and following the video demonstrations taught me that it is never too late to start drawing. With the skills I have learned through the book's fun and playful exercises, I am fulfilling a lifelong dream of drawing regularly and with confidence!

Andrew Valentine
Attorney

The Joy of Drawing book gave me a new insight into myself. Drawing is about how the artist themselves see things. The exercises in the book and accompanying video demonstrations allow you to explore at your own pace. It is totally worthwhile to do them. Spread your wings. It's art!!

Sherry Pang
Health & Welness Professional

Caroline Mustard is an exemplary teacher! I've been in the education business for sixty years, so I know how to recognize one by now.

John Mullen
Educator

I learned not to be afraid. Not to be afraid of failure or the fact that I'd never drawn before. Caroline and Katy made me understand that everything I was drawing was art and every line was just the way it was supposed to be and that I could get even better with practice. They helped me break a lot of personal fear of failure barriers.

Karen Kotoske
Non Profit Foundtion Executive

ABOUT THE AUTHORS
Two Brits who love to draw

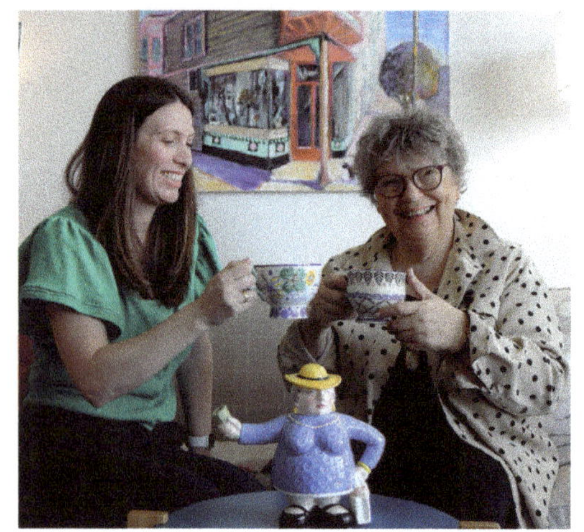

KATY LEA (Left) holds a BA in Fine Art (textiles) from Winchester School of Art in England. After graduating, she worked in London at a number of prestigious craft organizations and galleries, curating exhibitions and assisting artists, including renowned sculptor Sokari Douglas Camp, CBE and textile artist Ann Sutton, MBE. Katy went on to work as a project manager for cultural placemaking agency Futurecity in London. Currently she loves to teach people, young and old to hone their creative and drawing skills. She has a passion for interior design and is currently renovating her 1970's home in Los Gatos, California.

CAROLINE MUSTARD (right) graduated with a B.A. in Fine Arts from Brighton Art College in the UK. Leaving the UK in her 20's, traveling to Canada and then onto California to live while working in the fields of Graphic Design and Marketing. Caroline retired to Silicon Valley to be close to her older son and family who gifted her an iPad for her birthday. She quickly became obsessed with digital art and went on to find success as a professional artist, accepting commissions and exhibiting widely in the local bay area. Her colorful, expressive work mirrors her love of life. She is the co-founder of the Mobile Art Academy, a company dedicated to empowering users to learn and explore the world of digital art on their mobile devices. In teaching she found a calling to inspire others to draw and paint. Caroline lives in San Francisco.

CONTACT & CONNECTIONS
Website | Email | Links

WEBSITE: https://www.thejoyofdrawing.org

E-MAIL: thejoyofdrawingbook@gmail.com

MAILING ADDRESS:

The Joy of Drawing Inc.,

298 Westhill Drive,

Los Gatos. CA 95032

FACEBOOK: The Joy of Drawing Club

INSTAGRAM: @thejoyofdrawing_

YELP: The Joy of Drawing

YOUTUBE: @TheJoyofDrawing

YOUR NEXT BOOK
The Magic of Perspective gives you the skills of using perspective in your drawings
Order through www.blurb.com

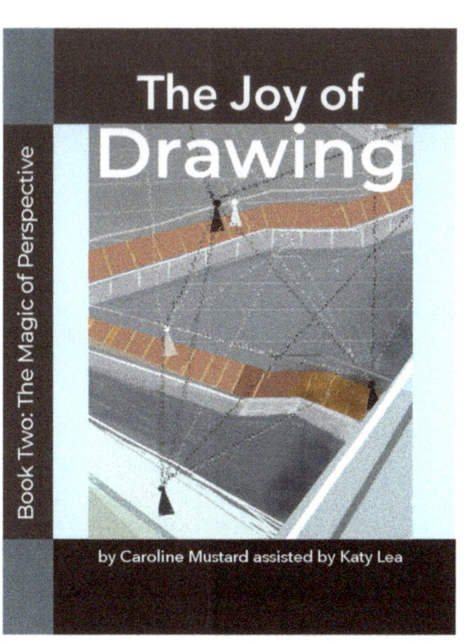